DAY TRADING SWING & FOREX FOR BEGINNERS

A CRASH COURSE TO INVEST IN THE STOCK MARKET:

MAKING A LIVING BY BUYING AND SELLING STOCKS, OPTIONS AND CURRENCIES,

AND USING PASSIVE INCOME STRATEGIES

Table of Contents

TRADE

Introduction

It is near impossible to predict market movements, and that is why day traders, swing traders, and forex traders place trades of any length in which they take a position with the hope that the price will move favorably for them. Day trading, swing trading, and forex trading can all be profitable in the long term if done correctly. Give one or more of these strategies a try!

Day Trading

Day trading involves making short-term trades on assets such as stocks or currencies with the goal of making a quick profit when you buy an asset and sell it at a higher price before its value decreases. To do this, day traders generally enter a position and then exit it if the price does not move in their favor. In the long term, day trading can be profitable for traders who know what to do to make correct trades at optimal times and avoid losing money due to falls in the stock market. Day trading can be very high risk, and taking excessive risks can lead to devastating losses over time.

Swing Trading

Swing trading involves taking a position in an asset over a longer period of time (ranging from days to years). When a swing trader first enters a trade, it is called a long position because they will be holding the asset for some time. If the price does not go up or down in their favor, they will be happy with their profit or loss. But if the price increases significantly by the end of the time frame, then they are considering taking an opposite position by selling the shares or contracts at that point. This strategy takes more effort and can take more than one year to make money, but it also has less risk than day trading.

Forex Trading

Forex trading involves buying and selling currencies. The market is open 24 hours a day, so it is possible to trade on the short-term fluctuations in the market. Just as with stocks, currencies can be more volatile than others at times. A successful forex trader should be able to identify trends, determine their risk tolerance and time frame for trades, manage risks accordingly, and be able to stick with a plan through thick and thin.

Day Trading VS. Forex Trading VS. Swing Trading

Before I go any further, let me define what these terms mean. The most basic concept is that they refer to the same groups of conditions. But to be clear, Forex involves currency trading; day trading involves the buying and selling of stocks or futures; swing trading involves both stocks and futures.

The average Forex trade takes about 40-60 days to make money on a short-term basis (2-4 weeks). It might take even longer if the market is moving too fast or if it's in a tight range for too long. A long-term trend will generally move at a faster pace than short-term trends.

If you are going to day trade, then I recommend day trading the trend. Always trade what the trend is doing. I can make more money on a trend than on a range, and while I was trading in one of my previous blogs, I had a 15-year streak of daily winning trades where my little brother could not beat me. I made money. It might be different in your account but it makes sense that the following something works better than trying to anticipate and trade against it (when you should never do that).

Swing trading is in between and generally involving very few trades. I've noticed that swing trading sometimes takes a longer time than day trading due to the fact that you are not looking for explosive moves up or down, but a slow gradual move. But it can be done much quicker than forex if the market is volatile, so keep that in mind.

Here's where trend following comes in. Momentum begets more momentum, while range-bound markets are very hard to trade in the short term because there's nowhere to go but up or down when the range is too small.

Day trading is a versatile strategy that can be used to earn a profit without taking any risk. For example, traders can buy a stock and hold it for several weeks to months in order to collect dividends or sell short.

Swing traders are generally more risk-averse than day traders because they are not trying to capture small gains; instead, they aim at higher profits over longer time periods. Investors who are willing to take the time to learn how to swing trade from the start will likely be rewarded in the long term.

What You Will Discover in This Book

I am a straightforward guy, so you will find that I like to get right to the point. There will be no beating around the bush. I will not spout out terms at you like this is a textbook. All the words in this book are meant to be understood by a complete newbie.

Before we get to these explanations, one thing needs to be stated: day trading is a business. I will remind you that throughout this book, it's such an important thing to understand. Companies do not just spring up and become successful overnight, even though it sometimes appears that way to outsiders. Businesses take hours of devotion every day and months of behind-the-curtain work to become successful. In the case of day trading, it usually takes between 3 and 6 months of regular time and effort to get your feet firmly planted on the ground to see the results you want.

Trading is not a get-rich-quick scheme. If you do not have the time it takes to learn the business's ins and outs, this is not your career. In fact, you must commit the right amount of time, be able to handle a challenge or the excitement of an ever-changing career, and have the will to learn and grow.

It is possible to make money through all three of these strategies, but it takes practice and knowledge. If you like the idea of any of these three methods, it is important that you practice your trading strategy and learn more about technical analysis. Technical analysis involves examining past price behavior to predict future price movement.

With some determination and a lot of effort, you can be a successful trader in any of these fields.

This book will discuss these three strategies, and how they are related to one another.

Are you ready to be serious about gaining new tools and skills that will allow you to take control of your financial future? If so, then read on! I promise that this book will let you hit the ground running with day trading, even though you are starting with zero knowledge and experience.

Don't wait and miss out on the opportunity to take control of your finances and your life. Procrastination will keep you chained to financial slavery. Read this book in its entirety to see how YOU can be the master of your destiny!

We have a lot of ground to cover in a few pages. So, let's get started.

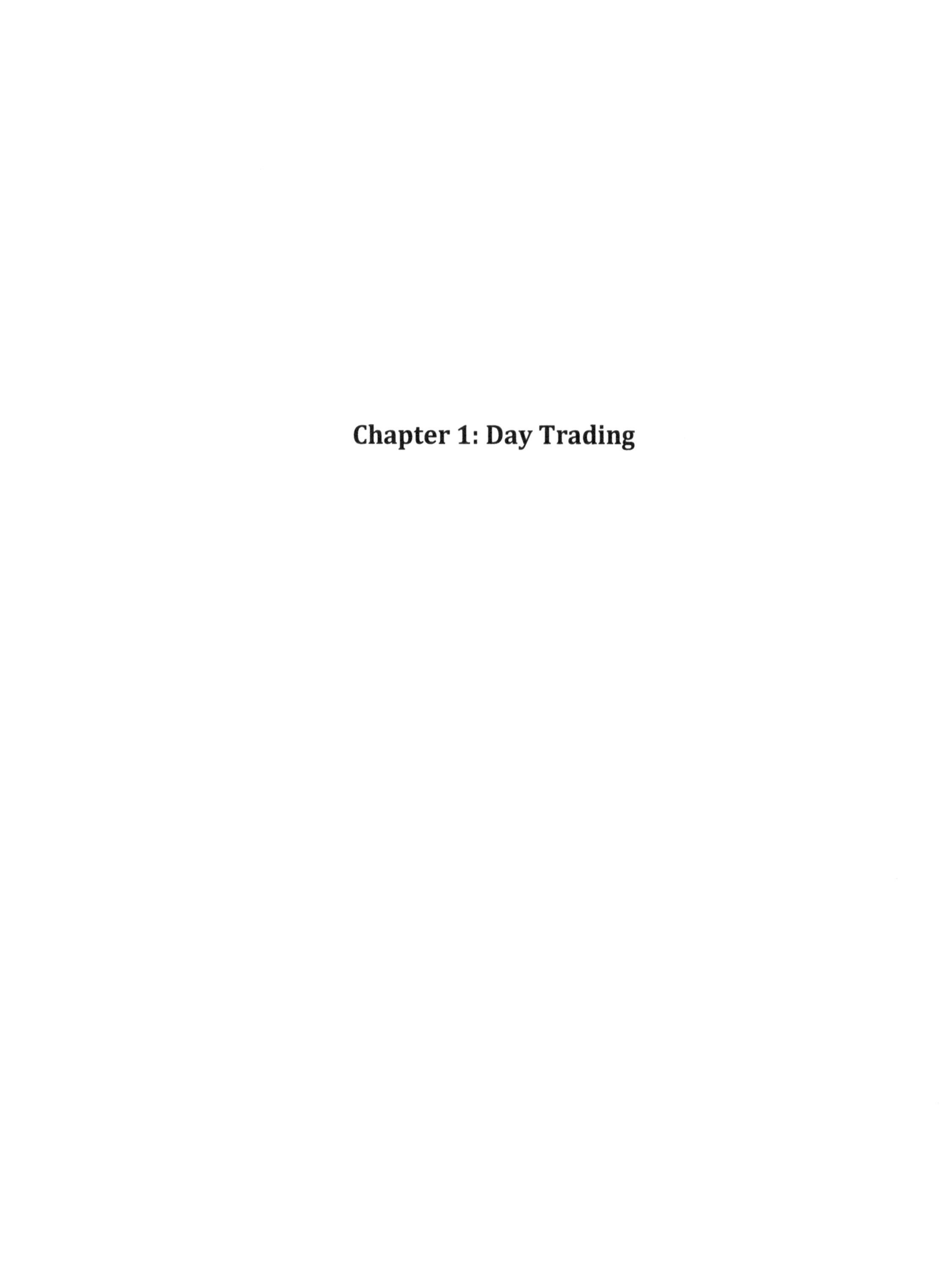

Chapter 1: Day Trading

What Is Day Trading?

The stock market is a vast place and there are millions of trades that take place all over the world, within a single day. There are both buyers and sellers in the market, and they will all have the same motive in mind; to increase their wealth potential.

Of all these trades, not everything will be of the same nature. Some will be long-term investments and some short. Long-term investments refer to those that are held for a long period of time. They are preferred by those who are not in a hurry to make money. Short-term investments, on the other hand, are those that are liquidated within a short period of time. They are not intended to be held for a long time, as owners will be interested in disposing of them early.

Short-term investments can be of many types based on the time that they are held. Some can be held for a month, some for a week, and some will be disposed of on the same day. This book will focus on the last option.

Better known as Intraday trading, day trading is one of the most preferred ways to trade in the stock market. Preferred mostly by those willing to part with their investment within a single day and realize a profit, or loss, from.

Intraday traders are interested in realizing a profit by capitalizing on the difference in the rates of these securities as opposed to long-term investors who will be in it for the Dividends.

Dos of Day Trading

Risk Capital

You have to understand that the stock market is a very volatile place, and anything can happen within a matter of a few seconds. You have to be prepared for anything that it throws at you. In order to prepare for it, you have to make use of risk capital. Risk capital refers to money that you are willing to risk. You have to convince yourself that even if you lose the money that you have invested, then it will not be a big deal for you. For that, you have to make use of your own money and not borrow from anyone, as you will start feeling guilty about investing it. Decide on a set number and invest it.

Research

Before you invest in the market, you need to research it thoroughly. Don't think you're going to learn as you go along. That is only possible if you at least know the basics. You have to remain interested in gathering information that is crucial for your investments, and it will only come about if you put in some hard work towards it. Nobody is asking you to stay up and go through thick texts books. All you have to do is go through books and websites and gather enough information to help you get started on the right foot.

Diversification

You have to stress diversification in your portfolio. You don't want all the money to go into the same place. Think of it as a way to increase your stock's potential. You have to choose different sectors and diverse stocks to invest in. you should also choose one of the different types of investments as they all contribute towards attaining a different result. Diversification is mostly seen as a tool to cut down on risk, and it is best that you not invest any more than 5% in any one of the securities.

Stop Loss

You have to understand the importance of a stop-loss mechanism. A stop-loss technique is used to safeguard an investment. Now say, for example, you invest $100 and buy shares priced at $5 each. You have to place a stop loss at around $4 in order to stop it from going down any further. Now you will wonder as to why you have to place the stop loss and undergo one. Well, by doing so, you will actually be saving your money to a large extent. You won't have to worry about the value slipping further down and can carry on with your trade.

Take a Loss

It's okay to have losses from time to time. Don't think of it as a big obstacle. You will have the opportunity to turn a loss into profit. You have to remain confident and invested. You can take a loss on a bad investment that was anyway not going your way. You can also take a loss on an investment that you think is a long hold and will not work for you in the short term. Taking a few losses is the only way in which you can learn to trade well in the market.
These form the different dos of the stock market that will help you with your intraday trades.

Don'ts of Day Trading

No Planning

Do not make the mistake of going about investing in the market without a plan in tow. You have to plan out the different things that you will do in the market and go about it the right way. This plan should include how much you will invest in the market, where you will invest, how you will go about it etc. No planning will translate to getting lost in the stock market, which is not a good sign for any investor.

Over Rely on Broker

You must never over rely on a broker. You have to make your own decisions and know what to do and when. The broker will not know whether an investment is good for you. He will only be bothered about his profits. If he is suggesting something, then you should do your own research before investing in the stock. The same extends to emails that you might receive through certain sources. These emails are spams and meant to dupe you. So, don't make the mistake of trusting everything that you read.

Message Boards

You have to not care about message boards. These will be available on the Internet and are mostly meant to help people gather information. But there will be pumpers and bashers present there. Pumpers will force people to buy a stock just to increase its value, and bashers will force people to sell all their stocks just because they want the value to go down. Both these types are risky, as they will abandon the investors just as soon as their motive is fulfilled. So, you have to be quite careful with it.

Calculate Wrong

Some people make the mistake of calculating wrong. They will not be adept at math and will end up with wrong figures. This is a potential danger to all those looking to increase their wealth potential. If you are not good at calculating, then download n app that will do it for you or carry a calculator around to do the correct calculations. The motive is to make the right calculations and increase your wealth potential.

Copy Strategies

Do not make the mistake of copying someone else's strategies. You have to come up with something that is your own and not borrowed from someone else. If you end up borrowing, then you will not be able to attain the desired results. You have to sit with your broker and come up with a custom strategy that you can employ and win big. These form the different don'ts of the stock market that will help you keep troubles at bay.

Chapter 2:Conservative Strategy of Day Trading

Awareness Is Power

Monitoring chief exchanging measures isn't sufficient. Informal investors likewise need to screen and stay up with the most recent occasions and news on the securities exchange considering the monetary viewpoint, rate plans, and the Fed's revenue.

In this way, achieve your home assignment. Draw up a list of must-dos of the stocks you might want to exchange and be constantly kept insider savvy of the overall business sectors, and chose organizations. Monitor business news and search for solid monetary sources.

Put Aside Funds

Gauge how much cash you need to roll the dice for each exchange. Various everyday brokers lose under 1% to 2% in their exchange accounts. For example, on the off chance that you hold a $40,000 exchanging portfolio and decide to lose 0.5 percent of your cash for each arrangement, the potential trade misfortune is $200 (0.5 percent * $40,000).

The overflow measure of monetary assets ought to be saved to exchange. You ought to consistently be prepared to lose them. Remember, it could conceivably occur.

Put Aside Time, as well

Day exchanging takes as much time as is needed, so that is the reason its name is day exchanging. Indeed, you should spend the fundamental piece of your day on it. Try not to try and take a gander at it if you are limited on schedule.

The exchanging method needs a dealer for all time to monitor the current circumstance available and to gauge spot openings, which can seize any time inside exchanging hours. On-the-spot choices are the key.

Get Started with Small

As a beginner merchant, focus on a limit of 1-2 stocks over the span of a meeting. Observing and searching for promising circumstances are all the more effective with a couple of stocks. These days, it is amazingly unavoidable to realize how to exchange with fragmentary offers, so you can explain explicit, more modest dollar sums you need to contribute.

Avert Penny Stocks

Likely you are chasing at exchanges and low costs yet avoiding penny stocks. Often, these stocks are illiquid, and the opportunity to hit a bonanza is hopeless.

The greater part of the stocks, valued under $5 per share, are de-recorded from the significant financial exchanges and may just be traded absurdly (OTC). Stay far from these until you have a specific opportunity to take care of your job.

Time Those Trades

At the point when financial backers and brokers put in the requests, they begin to carry out when the business sectors open up in the first part of the day, which prompts the unpredictability of a cost. An accomplished player can settle on a satisfactory decision and perceive examples to make benefits. Notwithstanding, it tends to be better for novices to peruse the market without taking any actions for the initial 15 to 20 minutes. Generally speaking, the center hours are less delicate. Accordingly, elements toward the end chime begin to go up once more. Albeit the times of heavy traffic guarantee openings, it's more secure for novices to deflect them interestingly.

Reduce Losses with Limited Orders

Tackle what sort of requests you will use to enter and leave exchanging. Is it accurate to say that you will utilize limit requests or market orders? At the point when you post a market request, it is executed at the most sensible cost available as of now — subsequently, the cost is ensured.
In the interim, a limited request guarantees the cost, however, not the execution. The restricted requests help you exchange all the more precisely, wherein you provide your cost estimate (not unreasonable but rather executable) for purchasing and selling too. More prepared informal investors may utilize alternatives techniques to ensure their positions as well.

Be Down-To-Earth Concerning Profit

To be worthwhile, a methodology doesn't have to win constantly. A ton of merchants just advantage 50-60% from their complete exchanges. Ensure that the danger for each exchange is restricted to a particular level of the record and that techniques for passage and exit are resolved and brought down unmistakably.

Keep Calm

There are events when the securities exchange evaluates your nerves. In the limit of an informal investor, you need to dominate the abilities to keep trepidation, eagerness, and expectation, under control. Your choices ought to be solemnly controlled by the presence of mind but not by feelings.

Adhere to the Plan

Prepared merchants need to act rapidly, yet not to think for quite a while. Why? Since they have a planned exchanging technique heretofore, close by the control to hold fast to that methodology. Following your recipe intently instead of attempting to seek after the benefits is additionally of an extraordinary significance. Try not to let your sentiments and feelings run over you, and put your arrangement away. Among informal investors, there's an expression: "Plan your exchange and exchange your arrangement."
We should consider a portion of the reasons why day exchanging can be so confounded before we jump into a portion of the intricate details of day exchanging.

Chapter 3:Advanced Strategy of Day Trading

When you are looking forward to capitalizing on the small frequent price movements, day trading strategies are the best for you. Any effective strategy that you will choose must be consistent and must rely on in-depth technical analysis that utilizes charts, market patterns, and price indicators predicting future price movements.

It is your responsibility to choose the most appropriate strategy that best fits your requirements. As a trader, it is good that you know the average daily trading volume.

Fallen Angel

A Fallen Angel is a strategy that involves a bond that has been reduced to junk bond status from an investment-grade rating as a result of the issuer's weakening financial conditions. In terms of stock, a fallen angel refers to a stock that has always been high and now has fallen considerably. Fallen angel bonds can be a sovereign, corporate, or municipal debt that a rating service has downgraded. The main reason for such downgrades could be attributed to revenue decline that generally jeopardizes the capabilities of issuers to servicing debt. The potential for downgrade often experiences a dramatic increase when expanding debts are combined with expanding debt levels. The securities of fallen angels are at times so attractive, particularly to contrarian investors who seek to capitalize on the potential. This enables the issuer to recover from the temporary setback.

Example:

Due to the ever-falling oil prices over several quarters, an oil company has reported sustained losses. The company, therefore, can decide to downgrade its investment-grade bonds to junk status as a result of the increasing risk of default. This will result in a decline in the prices of the company's bonds and, in addition, increase yields, which will make the contrarian investors to be attracted to the debt as they only see the low oil prices as a temporary condition. However, there are conditions where you are likely to go at a loss, especially when the fallen angel bond issuers do not recover. For example, if there is an introduction of superior products by a rival company, the issuers may fail to recover.

ABCD Pattern / Reverse ABCD Pattern

The ABCD pattern is a pattern that shows perfect harmony between price and time. ABCD pattern usually reflects the common and rhythmic style in the market movements. The geometric price/time pattern consists of three consecutive price trends with a leading indicator that can guide a trader to determine when and where to enter and exit a trade. As a trader, ABCD Pattern can be very important in identifying the available trading opportunities in any market (be it futures, forex, or stock) on any timeframe (be its position, intraday, or swing), and in any market condition (be it range-bound, bullish or bearish markets). Before placing a trade, ABCD Pattern can help you determine the reward and the risks of trade.

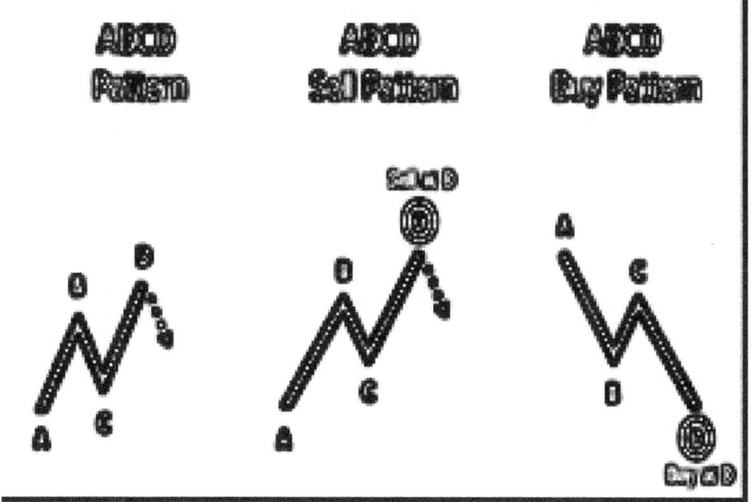

A representation of the ABCD Pattern (Above)

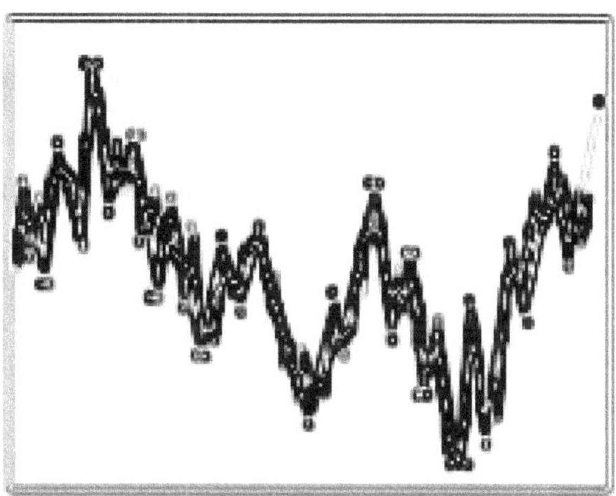

ABCD pattern on a trading chart

Bull Flag and Bear Flag

With technical analysis, a flag refers to a price pattern that can explode and move within a shorter timeframe to the prevailing price trend that has always been observed in longer time frames on a price chart. With the flag patterns, a trader can identify the possible prevailing trend that is continuing from a given point where the price has drifted against the same trend. Therefore, in the case that the trend resumes, by noticing the flag pattern, there will be a rapid price increase, and this makes the timing of a trade advantageous. Flags are areas of tight consolidation in price actions, and they show a counter-trend sharp directional movement in price. This pattern has 5 to 20 price bars.

Bullish Flag Formation

These are formation patterns observed in stocks that have a strong uptrend. Bull flags got their names from the fact that the pattern closely resembles a flag on a pole. A vertical rise in stock results in a pole, and a period of consolidation results in a flag. The flag is usually angled down away from the trend that is prevailing but also can be a horizontal rectangle. The bullish flag pattern starts with a strong price spike that is almost vertical. The prices then peaks and forms an orderly pullback where the lows and the highs become almost parallel to each other, making them almost form a tilted rectangle.

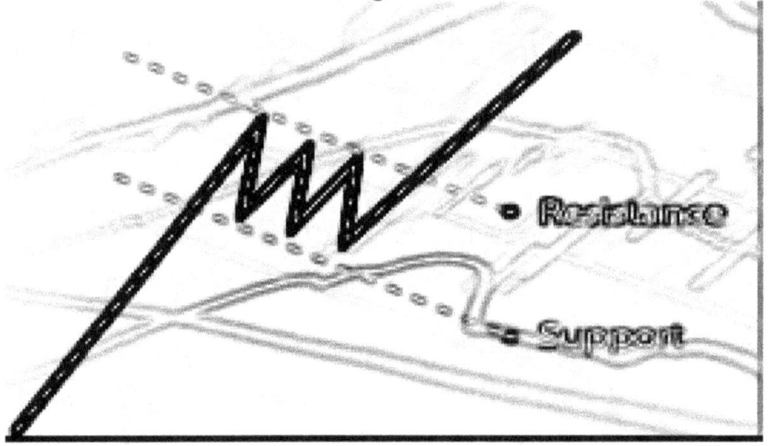

Bullish Flag Formation

The parallel diagonal nature is reflected by the plotted trend lines (both lower and upper trend lines). The breaking of the upper resistance trend line forms the first breakout. Another uptrend move and a breakout are formed when there is an explosion of the prices, causing prices to surge back towards the high of the formation.

Bearish Flag

The bearish flag is an inverted version of the bull flag. In this case, an almost vertical panic price drop is formed by the flagpole because the sellers make the bulls get blindsided and, as a result, there is a bounce having parallel lower and upper trend lines, forming the flag. The panic sellers are triggered when the lower trend lines break.
 This flag is similar to the bull flag in that the severity of the drop on the flagpole will determine how the strength of the bear flag can be.

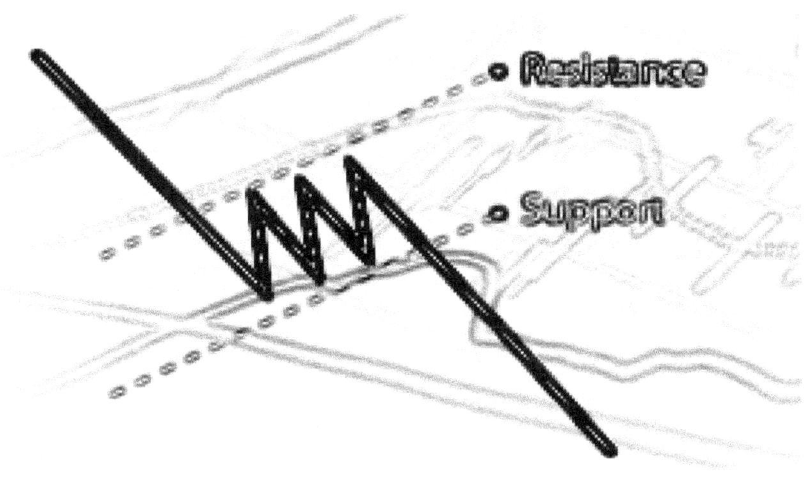

The Bearish flag

Develop Trading Skills

To become a trader, you are required to not only know about just finance or business but also hard science or mathematics. You must be an individual who can do deep research and analysis that can mirror the economic factors from a broader perspective, as well as the day-to-day chart patterns impacting different financial markets. As a trader, it is crucial that you need to sharpen your ability to concentrate and focus, especially in a fast-moving environment containing different people with different goals and ideas. You must also be able to practice self-control and regulate your emotions even when in situations upsetting you. Lastly, you should always be able to keep an accurate record of your trades to check on your account and to provide you with a learning opportunity that will help you become a better trader.

Chapter 4:Typical Beginner's Errors in Day Trading

Lack of a Plan

While trading, it is important that you have a plan. A plan acts as a compass direction while trading; it shows you the move that you should take to ensure that it is a wise trade decision. In a plan, we have different goals while trading. Some of these goals make our investment in day trading worth our while. They give us hope to achieve more out of life and, at the same time, inspire us to push beyond our abilities. A person's failure to create a plan results in failure. You find that you make investments without properly evaluating all the underlying factors. In case there are some risks involved, you find that you are not aware of them. In turn, these risks exposed you to the possibility of encountering a loss. When such incidences occur, you are not well-prepared with risk management strategies since you failed to have a plan. It goes without saying that a plan will help you achieve a lot in the trading industry. Most of the time, it provides a bearing for the direction that one is taking while trading.

The biggest challenge comes when you are a beginner, and you do not know much about trading. At that point, it is very easy to make a mistake. Any slight move that you take matters and has a big impact on your future. A single move can either sabotage what you have built for years or make you stronger than you were before. We have seen people succeed at trading, and then, at one point, they lose all that they have worked hard to build. Your success in this industry is dependent on the plans that you have regarding your trading future. Any slight mistake will cause you to go down faster than you could climb up. As you trade, you may come to a point where you encounter a series of wins. Such incidences make you feel confident in trading, and, at some point, you may be deceived to think that you can easily achieve success. At that point, you may decide to do away with having a plan. Such simple decisions can make a huge change in your trading, and you end up making a loss that you may not be able to recover from.

Trading to Cover Up for Previous Losses

Most traders are victims of this strategy. After conducting your daily trades, things may not move as planned. You find that you might have expected to get a profit out of the trades made, but instead, you end up with a loss. To cover up for the losses, you decide to engage in another trade, hoping that things will be different. Contrary to your expectations, you end up encountering more losses than you would have imagined. It gets worse if you spent more money on that investment as compared to the previous investments. You get to a situation where you are full of regrets due to the wrong decision that you made. It is important to note that rushed decisions barely lead to anything good. In most cases, they end up in sabotage, and you may not be able to recover from some of these incidences. We ought to learn that two wrongs do not make a right. Once you have made a mistake, the first step does not involve bouncing back to the same thing that caused you to make a mistake. You need to calm down and identify where you went wrong and start reorganizing from that point.

At times, we keep trading even after we make losses because we are in denial. You find that you are in a phase where you find it difficult to admit that you can make a mistake. These difficulties, at times, arise due to the fact that we have high expectations. Anything that does not lead us to achieve the dreams we created for ourselves automatically makes us regret the decisions that we made. At that point, one becomes frustrated since things are not moving as planned. Instead of taking some time off to realize where you went wrong in the previous trade, you immediately engage in another without carefully thinking it through. This is perhaps one of the biggest mistakes that most traders make. While it is good to have big dreams and ambitions, it is important that you do not make wrong decisions while trying so hard to achieve some of these dreams. Well, since the whole point of investing is earning more from the investments that we make, it may not always be the case. Some days, we will encounter some losses, and they should not lead us in making rush decisions.

Overtrading

As a beginner, you may have started trading with huge expectations. You have this big dream of becoming an overnight success. You decide to invest heavily in your trades, especially after hearing what other traders are earning out of trading. Ideally, it is healthy to have self-belief and imagine that you, too, can get to the point that other investors have reached. While at it, it is essential that you have practical dreams that are achievable. Some people have managed to sell out the idea that trading is an easy task that can result in earning within minutes. However, many people start trading and end up with huge frustrations when they fail to achieve their dreams as fast as experts. You find that with the excitement of engaging in trading, you end up engaging in multiple trades as a way to earn quick money. In this instance, most trade executions are not carefully planned; they are randomly selected. This means that you do not take time to come up with the right strategies to succeed in the different trades, and eventually, you end up losing.

At the same time, we have individuals who spread their risks across different trades. You are uncertain if you will end up making a loss or a profit. In this instance, you decide to spread your risks so that regardless of how the trade goes, you will not experience a total loss. In the beginning, this looks like an attractive strategy, and it almost feels like it is impossible to make a complete loss. However, you should remember that you are taking a gamble. This means that you can either earn a loss or a profit in both situations. It might occur that you experience a loss in all the investments that you made. In this case, that strategy will not benefit you in any way, especially since you still encounter a loss at the end. While coming up with the decision to conduct multiple trades, you need to be open to the idea that anything can happen. At the same time, you need to be well aware of the different option strategies that you can utilize while carrying out different trades. This allows you to remain focused and that you note some red flags before you end up making certain mistakes.

The Belief That a Big Investment Leads to Profits

Some people tend to have a misplaced belief that they need to make a big investment for them to earn a profit. This belief has caused a lot of individuals to make numerous mistakes while trading. We have had people invest a huge amount of their earnings, only to end up making a huge loss. For instance, you have $100 in your account, and you end up investing $90. With such an investment decision, you cannot afford to make a loss. Any wrong move can result in sabotage and make you lose what you worked so hard to get. At this point, with such an amount, you may end up feeling depressed after you have made a loss. Remaining with $10 can be challenging, especially considering that you had more, yet you lost it from making a trading mistake.

At this point, it is important that we learn to avoid placing all our eggs in one basket. In case of an accident, we may end up losing all the eggs and have none that is spared.

If you are a beginner, you should learn the importance of starting small. We find that most beginners are suffering from such decisions. You find that with the excitement of starting a new investment, you tend to overspend. This causes you to spend much of your time and energy on the new investment, and you barely take time to think things through. You end up making rash decisions that prove to be wrong later on, especially when things do not work in your favor. After experiencing a loss, you get to the point of self-realization that the move you took was wrong. We tend to have a misplaced perception that if we make a small investment, we equally receive small returns. Well, we have some trades that demand little from us and can result in huge incomes later on. We need to come to the point of understanding that the strategies that we utilize while trading can create a huge impact on our trading career. With a small investment and the right strategies, one can make a huge impact as they would make with a huge investment. At times, it all narrows down to the mentality that we have and uphold regarding different instances in life.

Ignoring the Expiry Date

Trades have a certain period where they are regarded as valid; after this period, the underlying stock becomes useless. You might have purchased some stocks and failed to be keen on the expiry date. Before you know it, you end up making a big loss after your stocks have been regarded as invalid. This is a sad way to lose the money that you have invested in your stock. To avoid being caught up in such, you need to watch the stock market carefully and make a move when it becomes favorable to you. This way, you avoid reaching the expiry date with nothing. To accomplish this, one way is to keep a record of your trades. If this is something that you keep referring to on a daily basis, it becomes difficult to overlook some of these things.

Lack of an Exit Plan

We are too fast in identifying the signals that lead us to engage in a certain trade, but we barely take time to identify when to exit a trade. This is a mistake that we end up regretting deeply. Mainly, if you engage in a trade, it is expected that you identify all the factors that can sabotage what you have built. At times, you find that one is in a position to earn a lot from a particular trade strategy. However, if they keep holding on to their position, they may encounter a loss. To avoid finding yourself in such situations, learn to note the signals that point out that you need to leave a given trade. Staying will make things worse, so exiting is the best solution at this point. At times, you might be betting on the possibility of making a huge profit or making a huge loss. In such times, you would rather exit the trade and earn a small profit than take the risk of staying. When you stay, you might not be sure if you will earn a huge profit or experience a huge loss. All of the above are some of the key mistakes that the majority of us make while trading. However, if you feel like you are already making some of these mistakes, there should be no cause for alarm. I will provide some guidelines on how you can avoid making these mistakes while engaging in day trading options. There are more mistakes that traders make that have not been highlighted. You can learn more about them from other platforms. After all, as a trader, learning is something that you have to embrace.

Chapter 5:Swing Trading

What is the Swing Trading?

Swing trading is indeed a form of trading that seeks to grab short to medium returns on a stock (or another financial instrument) over even a span of weeks or months. Swing traders mainly utilize fundamental analysis to search for trading possibilities. In order to assess cost patterns and trends, these traders could use significant analysis.

Money Required for Swing Trading

Let's look at how large an account you'd like to swing a trade for livelihood.
If someone advises you that someone wants $X to sell for a livelihood, they wouldn't realize what they really are speaking about.
Several factors determine how long it costs to swing a trade for livelihood, so it isn't easy to have a total amount that would appeal to us.
Here are all the key topics to understand:

- The basic life expenditures
- The standard of lifestyle people chooses to sustain.
- Who else do people support?
- How much would you like to save per month?
- What other costs will you have incurred by investing full-time (hospital services, etc.)?
- The effectiveness and benefit of your trading strategy.
- How are you going to deal with a trade recession?

The smartest thing you could do is get a stable income when you're learning to exchange. Build your assets from the trading revenue.
Once you are ready to generate 2-3 times the existing trading revenue, you should try swing trading on a full-time basis. When it becomes clear that you're wasting funds by heading to work, it's definitely time to leave your work and trade. Or perhaps not.
It would be best if you still held your career and even served part-time to provide a stable income stream. It depends on one's priorities, what they are comfortable doing, and the other responsibilities.
The easiest way to start is to monitor your expenditures. Remember to implement any protection to deal with emergencies. Perhaps you might not notice how much you're investing.

On the other hand, you do not know how minimal your monthly expenses are. If that's the situation for you, perhaps it would be simpler to substitute your earnings with trading. Often, swing trading means keeping a stake either longer or shorter for far more than a trading day, but normally not longer than a few weeks and months. It is a generalized timeline since certain trades can last much longer than a few months, but the trader could also deem them swinging trades. Swing trades could also occur on the day of a trading session, but this is an unusual scenario that is caused by highly unpredictable circumstances.

The aim of swing trading is to catch a fraction of a possible market shift. Although some traders are looking for dynamic stocks with a lot of change, others might choose more subdued stocks. In any way, swing trading seems to be the method of determining where the investment's price is expected to move ahead, entering a spot, and then gaining a portion of profit if the move suddenly appears.

Efficient swing traders are indeed trying to catch a fraction of the anticipated market change, and then carry on to the next chance.

Often swing trader's measure trading on even risk or reward basic principle. By studying the map of the commodity, they decide where they would reach, where they could put an end to the loss, and afterward predict where they should make a benefit. If they lose $1 per stock on the setup that might fairly generate a $3 profit that is a reasonable risk to reward ratio. On the other hand, actually, losing $1 to raise $1 or just earn $0.75 is not quite as beneficial as that.

Swing traders mainly use fundamental analysis owing to a short-term habit of the exchange. That being said, a critical approach could be used to improve the analysis. For instance, when a swing trader perceives a constructive setup in a portfolio, they might like to check that the dynamics of the commodity are either favorable or strengthening. Swing traders would also search for openings on regular charts and therefore will follow one hour or fifteen minutes charts to identify accurate admission, prevent loss, and take-for-profit amounts.

Swing Trade Strategies

Swing trader continues to search for multi-day graph trends. Many of the much more popular patterns include shifting average crossovers, triangles, cup-and-handle trends, flags, head and shoulder patterns. In relation to other markers, main reversal candlesticks could be used to develop a strong trading strategy.

At the end of the day, every swing trader formulates a scheme and tactic that brings them an advantage on certain trades. This includes searching for trading arrangements that aim to lead to stable fluctuations in the price of the commodity. It's not quick, and there's no technique or configuration that works every single time. With a desirable risk or reward, success is not expected at all times. The more amenable the risk to reward of a trading approach, the less necessary it is to succeed in order to generate net benefit over multiple trades.

The Real-World Example of the Apple's Swing Trade

The chart given above illustrates the time when Apple (AAPL) had a significant price increase. This was accompanied by the tiny cup and handle design that always signifies the continuity of the price increase if the stock shifts past the top of that handle.

In any case:

The price rises just above the handle, causing a potential purchase of about $192.70. One potential stop-loss location is under the handle, labeled with a rectangle, close to $187.50. It typically depends on entry and the stop-loss, the approximate trading cost is $5.20 for each share ($193.70-$186.50).
If you are searching for a possible payoff that is at minimum double the potential risk, every price over $204.10 ($193.70 + ($2 * $5.20)) would offer this.
Apart from the risk to reward ratio, the trader may also use other escape strategies, such as that waiting for a fresh low price. For this approach, the exit sign was not provided until $226.46, when that price fell far below the previous pullback level. This will have ended in the profit of $24.76 for each share. Think of another way — 12 percent benefit in return for much less than three percent uncertainty. This swing of trade consumed about two months.
Such escape approaches might be when a price is below the shifting average (never shown) or when the indicator, just as a stochastic oscillator, exceeds the signal point.

Pros and Cons

 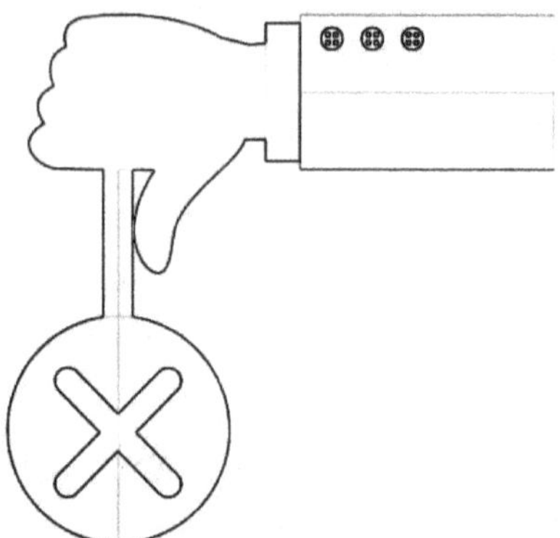

Swing traders typically keep a short to a long portfolio for at most a trading day but not longer than just a few days. This is a common time, but certain traders still prefer to keep positions indefinitely before their goal is met.

Swing trading is quite common with Forex retailers for two key factors. First, the Forex swing trade methods typically include entry and exit tactics that include a chart search just once or twice a day, and at most for some hours. This very flexible schedule is quite convenient for individuals with hectic lives and maximum work.

The core theory behind swing trading is to capture a bit of possible price fluctuation. Many swing traders favor higher-volatility assets (like foreign currency pairs), whereas others choose more stable market environments. In fact, swing involves purchasing lows and selling highs.

Anyhow, swing trading is mostly about forecasting the next market movement, getting into trading, and focusing on price movements. Productive traders aim to grab the only portion of the expected market shift and then search for another trading possibility.

Another bonus of swing trading is that you do not have to waste the whole week in front of screens when the business lasts for hours or days.

This method of trading is very common among successful traders pursuing short and medium trading with the aid of various forms of research. Technical assessment is the most critical method of analysis that can be used in swing trading due to the comparatively short-term length of the transactions. In addition, the fundamental review should be carried out in order to allow an even clearer evaluation. Swing traders are normally looking for trading options on 4-hour and regular charts. Effective swing traders aim to make small trades over the span of one month.

Swing trading enables you to gain the benefit of the normal rise and fall of the Foreign exchange markets. Stock markets rarely move in one direction indefinitely, and by being eager to draw advantage of all that, you would maximize your gains when you theoretically make profits as the Forex price increases for the next several days and afterward make more as that market pulls down, which it would inevitably do eventually. You could find more openings by being in or out of markets. If you glance at every financial map, you could notice that there seems to be often a clear long-term pattern, but the stock will not necessarily be in the region of support or opposition. By getting in or out of the market in a couple of days, you will (usually) collect money and locate other established platforms for other transactions. This helps you propagate the uncertainty around and link up quite a bit less money instead of always trying to step up with the margin for the latest positions when you discover new trades. By ending your first spot, you won't need to deposit any funds into your savings to fund the second position.

Stop setbacks are usually less than long-term transactions. The limit loss on swing trading may be 110 pips depending on a four-hour chart, while the stop loss on the weekly chart, depending on an overall pattern, may tend to be 500 pips. This encourages you to put broader positions rather than relatively poor leveraged positions by long-term patterns. You've got good limits. The swing trader is a much more complex trader and thus would usually have a particular region that they consider to be an indication that trading is going against them. That's why you understand precisely when the exchange doesn't work and can minimize the harm that poor trade could do. Longer-term traders typically have to lend themselves to the Forex market while they look for them all to "go for the fundamentals."

Some of the drawbacks of swing trading include that you will also get dragged down. That's because the market demonstrates support or opposition in a certain region, it does not guarantee that it will be rewarded today. Also, if you do a deal, you lose money. As a swing trader, you will have to take such risks quite often. You are likely to have setbacks periodically, regardless of how competitive you are. In the technical evaluation, you ought to be well-versed. It doesn't actually indicate "drawback," but it means hard effort. Usually, everyone can see the pattern on a chart that is moving from the bottom left to top right with time, so anybody attempting to swing the chart has to locate the entrances and exits. That is something that technical research could do, so you have to understand it first. This is time taking, it requires a unique mindset than long-term investing, with more ease. Although not generally scalping, swing traders face the risk of getting "startled out of stocks" when pullbacks in all of these narrower ranges tend to be much more aggressive than those staring at the weekly map. It is the psychological condition that several traders will inevitably have to struggle with throughout their careers.

Chapter 6:Conservative Strategy of Swing Trading

LONG TERM
INVEST
BUY SELL
SHORT TERM
HOLD

Keep it Simple

You may have heard of the term "paralysis by analysis." This happens when you analyze something to the point where you cannot make a decision. Some swing traders overcomplicate their analysis of security by using multiple indicators that all have to line up for them to enter a trade. In real life, everything does not often line up perfectly and you have to go with what you feel is right.

I have thus far covered many different tools and indicators you can use to help you to make a decision. You do not need to use all of them to be a successful swing trader. Once you find 1 or 2 that work well for you, you should then stick with those. If you decide to use a few different tools that all need to align, it will likely mean that you are not going to be trading very often. That is not necessarily a bad thing though. It is better to sit on your hands and wait for a good trade versus jumping in and out of marginal trade setups and slowly lose your money. The only one who wins, in that case, is your broker, as they collect fees for all of your trades (the successful ones and the losing one's).

Find several indicators that work well for you and focus on using them. Don't trade often, but trade smart, by knowing why you are entering a trade and, most importantly, knowing your risk to reward ratio and exit price points. As you gain more experience in swing trading, you will be able to better recognize trades that are going to work out even if everything is not perfectly aligned.

Having said this, when you do happen to find a number of indicators that are all aligned with the trade you are considering taking, it can certainly provide some level of confidence that you have a potentially profitable trade.

Treat your Swing Trading Activity Like a Serious Business

Should you decide that swing trading is a right fit for your personality, and that it is able to fit into your life along with all of your other interests and responsibilities, then you need to treat this activity as a very serious business. It will require an investment of time and effort, which hopefully will lead to some very good rewards.

Have a designated area where you do your research and keep all of your records. You are essentially becoming a professional money manager for yourself, so you should keep your work organized at all times. Everything you do with your business should be oriented toward making sure you are a success. If you feel like a professional, then you are more apt to trade like one.

Develop a Work Plan

Have a work plan and stick with it. Your work plan should include checking the market at the open and before the close. During this time, you should monitor your positions, set alerts and possibly enter orders at target levels that you think might get filled during the trading day.

I also recommend that you review your portfolio and market performance every night from Sunday to Thursday to ensure your assumptions about your positions and portfolio are still valid. On the weekend, you should try to do a more thorough review.

It is important to establish a work plan and keep it consistent. By keeping your work plan relatively consistent, you can measure your performance without introducing additional variables. Measuring your performance allows you to find areas to improve and make changes as you see fit.

Actively Manage Your Risk to Reward Ratio; Focus on the Entry

As a swing trader, your first and most important tool is your capital or cash. As I have said before, without cash, you cannot be a trader. I have written at length already about the necessity of assessing the risk to reward ratio on every trade and also on how much capital you should put into each trade. Following your rules on these points will prevent you from quickly losing all of your capital. You will be wrong on your trades some of the time and you need to make sure you live to trade another day.

Just planning and knowing your stop-loss and profitable exits are not enough for swing trading. Your entry becomes the next important step in your trade. You have already determined your stop-loss point and your target price(s) for a profitable exit. However, you calculated the risk to reward ratio based on an assumed entry price point.

Let's assume you found a good setup during a scan in the evening after the market has closed. The security closed the day at $10.50, and you see an upside to $12.00 with support at $10.00 where you would stop out. Therefore, you have a potential $0.50 loss compared to a $1.50 gain to the upside. That is a 1 to 3 risk to reward ratio, which is very good, and you are ready to pull the trigger and place a buy order in the morning. The market opens the next morning and the security you are ready to buy opens up at $11.00. What do you do? The novice trader is already invested mentally in the trade, so they buy. Unfortunately for them, their risk to reward is now 1 to 1, with the downside to $10.00 and upside to $12.00. This is no longer a good trade at that entry point.

The rational trader reassesses the situation. They may put a buy order in at $10.50, hoping to catch the entry they wanted on the security during the normal daily price gyrations in the market. This will give them the risk to reward ratio that they need to make a good swing trade. If they do not get a fill, then they need to reassess again, and maybe move on to finding another trade with a more appropriate risk to reward ratio. The bottom line, do not get emotional and chase a trade. The "fear of missing out" can motivate you to make a bad trade and you should be aware of this when picking your entry price on a trade.

Measure Your Results and Adjust Accordingly

As a trader, you must track your results to measure your performance. Nothing gets improved that does not get measured first. Every trader should use a tool to record the different aspects of each trade, from initial assessment through to the risk to reward expected, the entry point, and, finally, the exit. The tool can be a spreadsheet, it can be done on paper or it can be web-based. It does not matter how you do it as long as the process allows you to track the details of each trade as well as your performance.
Once you have your trades recorded in detail, you can go back at any time and review how the trade worked. You can compare your performance using the different indicators, i.e., is one working particularly well versus the others you use? Are you getting good entry points on your trades or do you need to exercise more patience? Are your exits working or are you consistently exiting a trade too early and not getting all of the money you could on a profitable trade? Are you respecting your stops?
Having all of this information to review will help you adjust your trading process and plan accordingly to maximize your performance without letting emotion enter into your decision-making.

Chapter 7:Advanced Strategy of Swing Trading

To become a perfect trader using the swing style, the major thing you need to know is how to identify any potential trade. When you have identified such trade, you can now begin to apply the various concepts that we have covered so far in this book. The steps we have given here are simply to show you how to apply all concepts you have learned so far. You can easily use some of these approaches to quickly execute and identify trade as well as direct potential traders to the techniques.

Sizing Up the Market

Any swing trader should definitely know more or less about the market; to be a complete trader, you should know about the currency market, state of equity, fixed income, etc. You need this because hardly will you find any market that is not related. So, if there is an increase in the prices of a currency, you should expect that there will be a bear market in the case of bond prices. There will almost be an immediate flaw in equity if the bond price keeps falling rapidly. Commodity prices go up if the dollar weakens. We can continue to show how all these things are related.

The main thing is that you will be able to improve your trading ability when you look at all these major markets; this will allow you to be able to predict the possible directions of any other market.

Identifying the Top Industries

There are numerous ways you can use to identify the leading industries. You can use the top 10 % list to identify the stocks on the long side of the market. You can make use of the High Growth Stock Investor (HGS Investor) software which is a better tool than focusing only on the top 10 %.

Ensure that you look out for swing trades that are promising in the industry group within the top 10 % for long candidates and the short candidates' lower 10 %. Doing this will make you know the leading group and you can easily select from the candidates within the top two industries.

Selecting Promising Candidates

Many traders opt for technical analysis when they are selecting promising candidates but it will be better to use the fundamental analysis first; this will facilitate easy selection of your promising candidate. Then, you can now use technical analysis to time your entries and exits.

- Screen securities: When you screen security, you are sure to have filtered out penny stocks and thinly traded securities. We recommend you use the format below to screen

Market capitalization ≥ $ 250 million
Average daily volume ≥ 100,000 shares
Stock price ≥ $ 5

- Access chart patterns and rank the filtered securities: You can easily rank filtered securities using the price to cash flow ratio or earnings rank. After that, you can access the charts of promising stocks.

Determining Position Size

Now that you may have found your trade, you may be having problems with allocating it. You will know by now that we recommend that you set your position by risk level rather than by percent of capital, this will easily allow you to get your position size through knowing your stop loss, and limiting losses level should usually be between 0.25 % and 2.0 % of the value of your account in case the security comes to the level of the stop losses.

Executing Your Order

Ensure that your swing trading time commitment is in consistency with your order entry. If you are a part-time swing trader, you can enter near the closing price by using the limit orders at the exact day the signal was generated. Full-time traders can buy at a better price if they add the intraday trading overlay.
It is important that you enter a stop-loss order as soon as you execute your trade whether you are a full-time or part-time trader, except you are a full-time trader who tries to watch your position during market hours every day.

Recording Your Table

Recording of your table should follow the execution of your trade. The recording serves to keep your journal up-to-date and you can easily find some helpful details there. This book has dealt with the information that your journal should contain. Ensure that you keep such information simple and always strike a balance so that you do not enter too much irrelevant detail.

Monitoring the Motion of Shares and Exiting at the Right Time

When you might have recorded your positioning in your journal, you should be keen on monitoring them and ponder on your best exciting strategy. We recommend that you use the following scenario to know when exactly to exit.

- When you see the position meandering sideways.
- When you notice that the position is unprofitable.
- When the position is profitable.

Enhancing Your Swing Trading Skill

We may have given you some insights into trading but keep in mind that no trading system works efficiently 100 % at every time, likewise, you cannot be 100 % perfect as a swing trader. Expect to lose but know the numbers of losses you can accommodate. One of the ways by which you can become an efficient trader is that you should try as much as possible to evaluate your journal every month; this will make you able to easily detect your winning and losing pattern of position.
You can then alter your trading pattern based on the winning or losing position, but do not change this often because of one or two losses that you may eventually work upon. If you lose hugely, then it is possible that you will not need to adjust your entry and exit strategy but rather your risk management strategy.

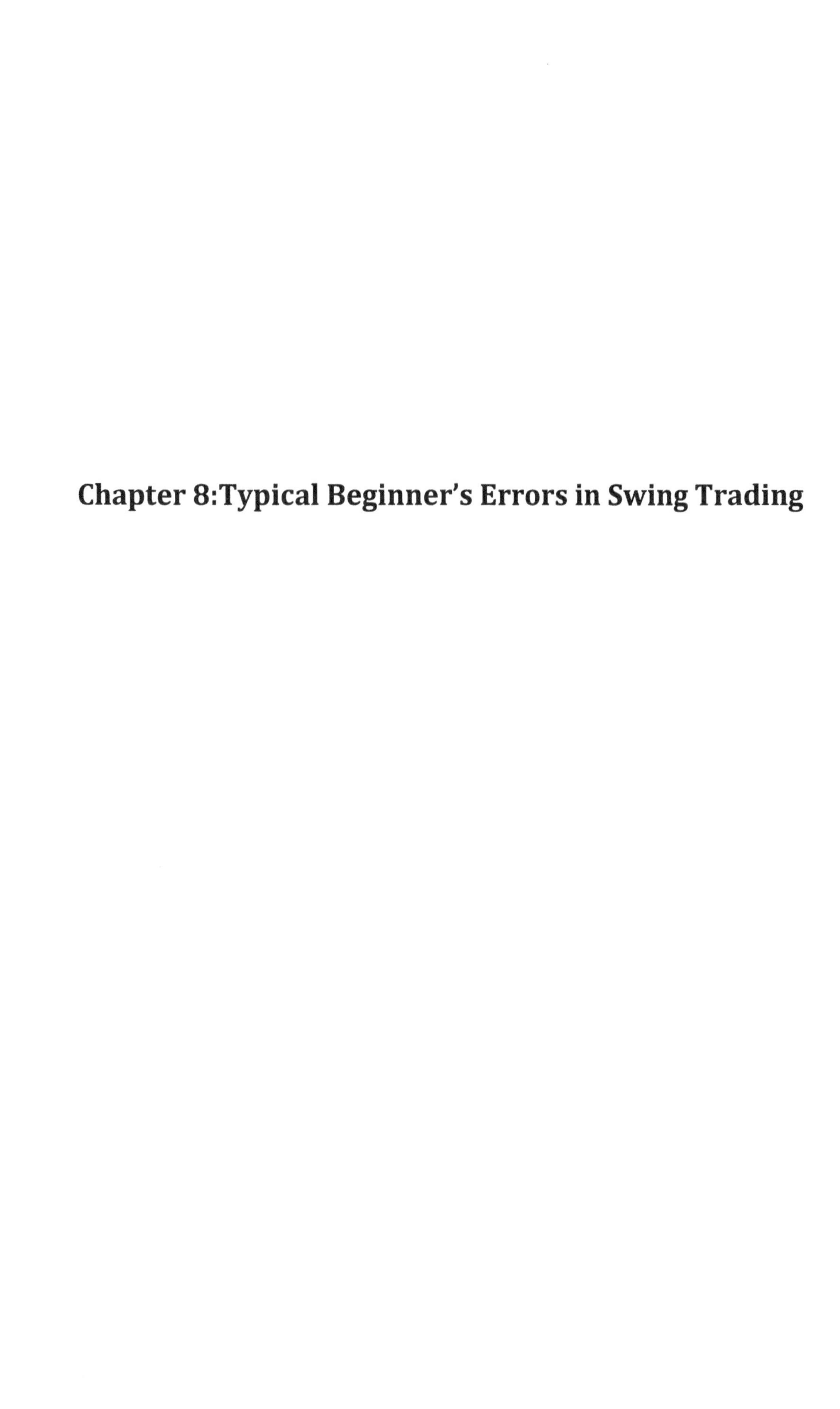

Chapter 8:Typical Beginner's Errors in Swing Trading

COSTS

Mistakes are always part of the game in any trade. Traders in swing trading also make mistakes that cause them to fail. Others commit mistakes due to ignorance of the different rules and strategies used in swing trading. This is all about giving details of the various mistakes committed by the different traders in swing trading.

Below are the various mistakes swing traders commit while trading:

Lacking a Trading Plan

Most of the traders starting off on swing trading lack a well-defined plan. What do you normally think of when you do this? Swing trading is a risky arena. You need to be well-armed and prepared before entering into trading. Lacking a proper trading plan makes you misbehave in your trading, which is a very bad idea.

You normally lack a trading routine when you fail to have a plan. You find yourself lacking the objectives and goals for your trading. A trading plan enables you to stick to the plan and work hard for your objectives. Failing to have a plan makes you do things when you feel like it is so risky in the swing trading environment.

A plan is basically composed of objectives and strategies. Without it, it is like going to a war with no weapons with you. Prepare yourself with a good plan to be able to know the risks involved in the market since it enables you to formulate your own trading strategies.

Lacking a Time Horizon for Your Trading

Always known as a swing trader the duration you have for investment reasons. It enables you to be aware of the time duration you have before expiry. When you select your time horizon to be until retirement, it tells that you have to invest for a while before the time of retirement.

Failing to Utilize the Stop-Loss Orders

Stop-loss orders are very crucial for all kinds of traders. You need to implement it for safety reasons during trading. A trader who fails to utilize stop-loss orders strategies ends up with huge losses on their trading. You find yourself making big losses that could be controlled.

Losses all times turn down the success of any business. Failing to arm yourself so well in trading is just a total failure for your swing trading. You need to be alert with the crucial strategies in swing trading so as to survive and succeed.

Lacking Control over the Trading Losses

Losses will normally occur in most businesses, but does that mean you should have no control over them? You need to make fast and efficient actions when losses occur in your swing trading, even the smaller losses. Ignoring the smaller losses will make them accumulate so hard, and time will reach you will have no control over them.

You need to be serious about the losses that come up and be able to handle them before they shut down, you're trading. Losses promote no growth in swing trading. You need to have policies with you on how to handle losses. Most of the traders neglect this mistake which makes them fail in swing trading tremendously.

Putting Much Trust in Financial News

Watching and following up on news is not a bad thing, however, you need to be extra careful with what you hear or come across online. Some bloggers mislead novice traders a lot on how to handle their trading. You should be alert with all the information. Some people just want to see fail. Do not apply all the information you hear from other people. Have your own ways of how to handle things in swing trading. You do not need to copy what others are doing, people have different abilities. Rely only on the trusted sources and swing trading forums. Consult the experts in swing trading for any information that you have heard and you are not sure about it. Have trust in yourself that your ways will also succeed in swing trading.

Working on Too Many Markets at Once

A high number of swing traders fail in their trading due to being over-occupied with too many markets at once. You are not like a robot machine; you need to decide on a reasonable number of markets that you can handle. Do not be greedy for money, you need to calm down and at least focus on a few and perfect your skills rather than being involved with too many markets.
This will make you get out of control. Concentrating on many markets is even not healthy for your body and mind. You do need to select every market. You should choose the ones you are highly interested in, perfect your skills on them, and ace swing trading.

Being Overconfident

Being a confident swing trader is a good thing, but being extra than that is really a poor thing to do. Overconfidence has killed the dream of many swing traders. Traders are normally over certain with what they are doing and fail to list down even the risks that may be involved in their trading. You need to remember both the worst-case and the best-case scenarios in swing trading while planning. Consult others when you need help with your strategies, you may learn a few things that will help you in your trading. Do not be that kind of a bold trader who does things alone with no trainer or some sort of master in swing trading. Do not trust yourself that much, you might be doing things the wrong way.

Lack of Patience

Good things take time. This saying is also relevant in our case here. Most traders have no patience at all with the huge profits. They only want money to be accumulated in the first days after joining swing trading. That is not possible unless all you want to accumulate are huge losses. You need to give yourself more time before you begin to earn more money.

The kind of traders who rush in trading for their greed for money end up nowhere. You need to be realistic sometimes to succeed in swing trading. Do not rush the trade, the money will keep coming. Do the right thing at the right speed. Do not implement too many strategies in your trading and get confused. Work with at least one successful trading strategy and relax.

Indiscipline

It is not advisable to be undisciplined in swing trading. Success is directly related to discipline. When you are disciplined in your trading, you are able to handle your trade with caution and with the right mindset. Traders who mix their trading procedures and activities with other things end up mixing everything up. You need to be aware of all of your strategies and objectives at your fingertips to be able to know what you want to achieve. Not being disciplined makes you even forget your targets and your policies. This, of course, leads to total failure in your trading.

Too Much Focus on Profit

Profit-making is one of the main objectives of all businesses, but why focus too much on profit and forget about other crucial factors in swing trading? Factors like risk management and loss handling losses also need attention. Do not be the kind of traders who just think of making a profit and end up making big losses in their trading.

You need to have a balance on how you handle your trading activities. Do not allow to accumulate high profits which have the same amount as losses. There will no earn since the losses made will decline both your trading capital and your profits.

Failing to Trust Your Abilities

You need to have trust in your capabilities. As a beginner, you should not compare yourself with the expert successful traders. This will make your esteem to decline. You need to be yourself and remind yourself that you will succeed. All you need to do is to comply with the strategies and objectives that you wrote down. You also need to learn a lot and do much research in swing trading in order to succeed.

Using Much Money on the Investment

The amount of money you are dedicating for investment should be a good amount of your disposable income that you can quickly or easily refund. Utilize a little money at the beginning to avoid huge losses. The higher the amount of money you use for swing trading, the higher the number of losses that can come up due to the many risks that are involved in swing trading. Most traders boast around with a huge amount of cash for trading and, unfortunately, end up making huge losses. Also, do not trade with your school fees or rent, you will have issues with your school finance.

Being Emotional on the Money Lost

Catching feelings in trading is not advised for any swing traders. Some traders give up when losses occur and decide to quit. Do not be a faint-hearted trader; you need to be strong that the money lost will get refunded. Stand strong and wish yourself good luck.

Being Too Much Aggressive

Most unsuccessful swing traders failed to succeed because of their aggressive behavior. Being aggressive makes you lose a lot of money which leads to the failure of swing trading. This normally happens on a bullish type of market. Relax, and everything will work out.

Laziness and Being Irresponsible

All types of trading are tough. You need to put much effort into your swing trading in order to widen your knowledge. Failing to do much research will not keep you informed and updated. You need to go with the trend. Do not be left behind. Failing to go through different newsfeeds on swing trading will enable you to be outdated.
Irresponsible swing traders who lack trading plans and strategies get confused and finally decide to quit swing trading. You need to be responsible and make decisions even during the worst-case scenarios. Do not fail to work even on the small losses that occur during swing trading. Trade responsibly, taking into account all the risks involved in swing trading.

Ignoring Risk Management Trading Strategies

What do you expect when you fail to implement the few strategies needed for risk management? Swing traders who fail to implement the risk management strategies of course end up being involved with too many risks. You need to check on the different swing trading strategies that exist and choose the best that handles risks in swing trading. This will protect your trading capital and also the amount of profit accumulated. Failing to arm yourself well enough will bring failure to your trading.

Implementing Many Small Moves

This mistake is normally committed by novice traders who make moves on any small changes in the market. You find yourself making trades even on your weakest points. There are high chances of big losses during this time. You need to be extra cautious and only make sure moves when relevant changes occur in the market. Small moves contribute to huge losses. Trade at the right time according to your trading plan. Avoid this mistake in order to succeed in swing trading.

Being so Close to the Market

Traders who focus so much on the swing trading market end up living in worries all the time. You end up putting much effort even on small things that need less attention. Do something else other than trading. You can even do some cooking or even water flowers. Give yourself some time to catch a breath with a good mindset that everything will work out well. Do not be so close to the market—you will worry too much for nothing.

Lacking a Swing Trading Strategy

Strategies are like guidelines that exist in swing trading to help you when making decisions. Most of the swing traders forget to formulate the trading strategies when formulating the swing trading plan. Lacking swing trading strategies is a very bad idea. Strategies help you in managing risks and accumulating more profit. Always stick to your working strategies that are according to your trading plan.

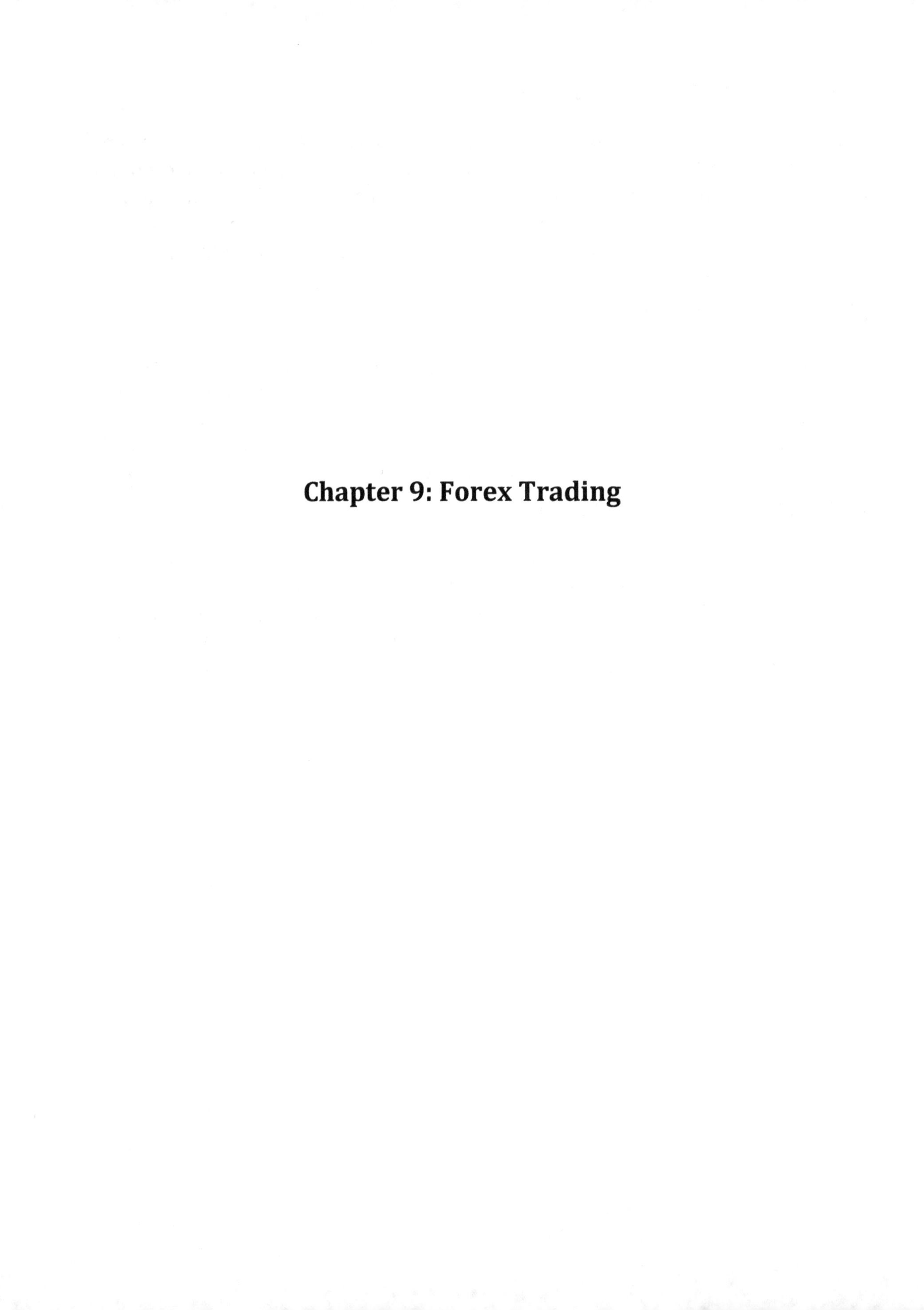

Chapter 9: Forex Trading

GBP/USD	82%	1.54260	14:15	04:23
EUR/JPY	82%	135.365	14:15	04:23
GBP/JPY	81%	183.543	14:15	04:23
USD/JPY	73%	118.983	14:15	04:23
USD/CAD	79%	1.25174	14:15	04:23
USD/CHF	79%	0.94890	14:15	04:23
EUR/GBP	78%	0.73751	14:15	04:23
AUD/USD	79%	0.77801	14:15	04:23
AUD/NZD	73%	1.03561	14:15	04:23
NZD/USD	73%	0.75125	14:15	04:23

Forex is commonly known as foreign exchange or FX, and it involves the buying and selling of different currencies with the aim of making profits based on the changes in the value. The forex market is the largest market in the world; it is larger than the stock exchange market. Therefore, it attracts many traders. There is high liquidity in the foreign exchange market, and as such, this attracts both experienced and beginner traders. In fact, the forex trade market is so large that all the stock markets in the world cannot match its capacity. The foreign exchange market is decentralized across the globe; therefore, all the different currencies in the world are traded freely.

Currency Pairs

There are very many types of currencies across the world, and all of them have three-letter symbols; for example, the Euros are EUR, American Dollars are USD, British Pounds are GBP, Swiss Francs are CHF, etcetera. The currencies have been majorly divided into two major and minor currencies. The major currencies involve these derived from the powerful economies in the world that are; the USA, the UK, Japan, the Eurozone, Australia, Canada, New Zealand, and Switzerland. These currencies create forex pairs with each other and with other minor currencies.
When one goes to a store to purchase some groceries or any other item, he/she needs to exchange one asset of value for another, for instance, milk for money. This applies to forex exchange too; buying and selling one currency for another. Every pair involves two currencies whereby one buys or sells the currencies against the other.
Forex pairs can be classified into three types, namely Major pairs, Exotic pairs, and Minor pairs. The major pairs always consist of the United States Dollar, and many people trade in them. The major pairs are USDCHF, USDJPY, EURUSD, AUDUSD, GBPUSD, NZDUSD, and USDCAD. The minor pairs involve all the currencies participating in the major pairs apart from the United States Dollar. They include CHFJPY, EURGBP, EURAUD, JPYAUD, NZDCAD et cetera. The exotic pairs involve one minor currency and one major currency, for instance, USDNOK, USDKSH, EURTRY, and so on.

How Does Forex Work?

Just like the stock markets, one can trade currencies depending on his/her prediction on the changes of value. The greatest difference between stocks and currency trades is that forex can trade down and up very easily. If one thinks that a particular currency will have a value increase, he/she may buy it, and if he thinks that the currency will fall, he /she may sell it. The forex market is so large that finding a buyer or seller is too easy compared to other trade markets. Let's assume that a trader hears reports that a country such as China will devalue its currency with the intention of drawing more foreign investors into the country. If he/she thinks that the devaluing trend will continue, the trader may sell the currency of China against another, for example, the USD. The more the currency of China devalues against the United States dollar, the higher the trader's profit. However, if the currency gains value against the US dollar, then the trader will have increased losses and may want to leave the trade as soon as possible.

Summarily, Forex trading involves placing a bet on the value of one currency against the other. Remember that in a pair, the first currency is the base while the second currency is the secondary or the counter. For example, in the EUR/USD the EUR is the base while the USD is the counter. If a trader clicks buy or sell, he/she is buying or selling the base. This means that if a forex trader thinks that the EUR will increase in value in contrast with the United States dollar, he/she will buy the EURUSD. If the trader thinks that it will drop, he/she will sell the EURUSD. If, for instance, the asking price 0.7060 and the bid price is 0.7064, and then the spread price is 4 pips. Whether the value of the EUR rises or falls, the trader will make a profit or loss once he covers the spread price. The spread price is usually higher for minor currencies.

Basic Terms in Foreign Exchange

In foreign exchange, the term 'Position' refers to a trade that is in progress, and it is basically classified according to the expectation of traders. The term 'long position' refers to the trade where the trader has purchased a particular Currency (the first in a pair) with the expectation that the value will rise. When the trader sells back the currency to the market (expected to be a higher price than the purchase price), the trade is complete, and the long position is "closed." A short position refers to the trade where a trader sells a currency (the first in a pair) with the expectation that the value will fall, and then he/she buys it back at a lower price. When the trader buys the currency back ideally for less than he/she sold it the trade is complete, therefore "closed."

The pair that is mainly traded in the forex market is the American dollar versus the Euro or USDEUR. The currency identified on the left side is referred to as the base currency, while the one on the right is referred to as secondary currency. The base currency is the one a buyer or seller wishes to buy or sell, while the second currency is the one a trader uses to make the transaction. Each trade pair has two prices, the bid and the buy. The 'bid' is the selling price of the base currency, while the 'ask' is the buying price. The difference between the bid and the asking price is referred to as the spread, and it indicates the amount that brokers charge to keep the position open. The spreads become narrower when more currency is traded when a currency has high volatility. If a pair is very rare, the spread will be wider.

Usually, the quote prices are presented with 4 numbers after the dot. In the case of EURUSD for example, the price might be 1.2589 to mean that for every Euro that a trader wishes to buy, he/she will have to put in 1.2589 US dollars. Changes occurring in the value of the currency will be seen on the last figure after the dot. It is mainly referred to as a pip. The gains, the losses, and the spreads will normally be indicated in pips. Another term commonly used in forex trading is going long, which means buying and going short means selling. A bullish trader normally predicts that the market will rise, while the bearish trader hopes that the market will fall to benefit. The term bull market indicates that the market will rise or increase, while the bear market indicates that the market will fall or decrease. Experienced traders normally base their decisions and strategies on market trends; therefore, they follow all the relevant events within the markets. The study of trends helps the traders to gain profit in the market.

Formally, traders had to call the brokers and inform them of the actions he/she should take in the market. However, technology has made it possible for many traders to transact directly using software referred to as a trading platform. There are many trading platforms available for the internet, computers and even phones. Every trader selects a platform that will work well with his/her trade strategy to reap maximum benefits. Leveraged trading, also referred to as trading on the margin is a process that allows the traders to hold larger positions than they can with their own fortune only. In a large number of forex pairs, a trader can hold maximum leverage of 400:1, which means that for every $400 the trader will invest $1. Consequently, if he/she wishes to purchase 100000 EURUSD at the price of 1.2674, instead of paying $126,740 he/she will pay 25 percent for the amount. One should remember that the losses and profits usually depend on the size of the position, and as much as leveraging trade can magnify the profits, it can also enhance losses.

Example:

Let's say a trader wants to transact in the forex market. He/she logs onto the trading platform and checks the bid and ask price. Assuming that he/she finds that the asking price is 1.2356 and the bid price is 1.2359; the pip will be 1.2356-1.2359= 3 pips. The three pips will go to brokers. If for instance, that trader believes that the Euro will rise, he will put a 'buy' command. He will then select a particular number of units he/she wishes to buy for instance 10,000. The normal price for that would be $12356, and if the trader is relying on leverage trading, he will pay $30.89. If the markets move up as the trader had indicated, say to $1.2360, then he/she will make a profit.

Chapter 10:Conservative Strategy for Forex Trading

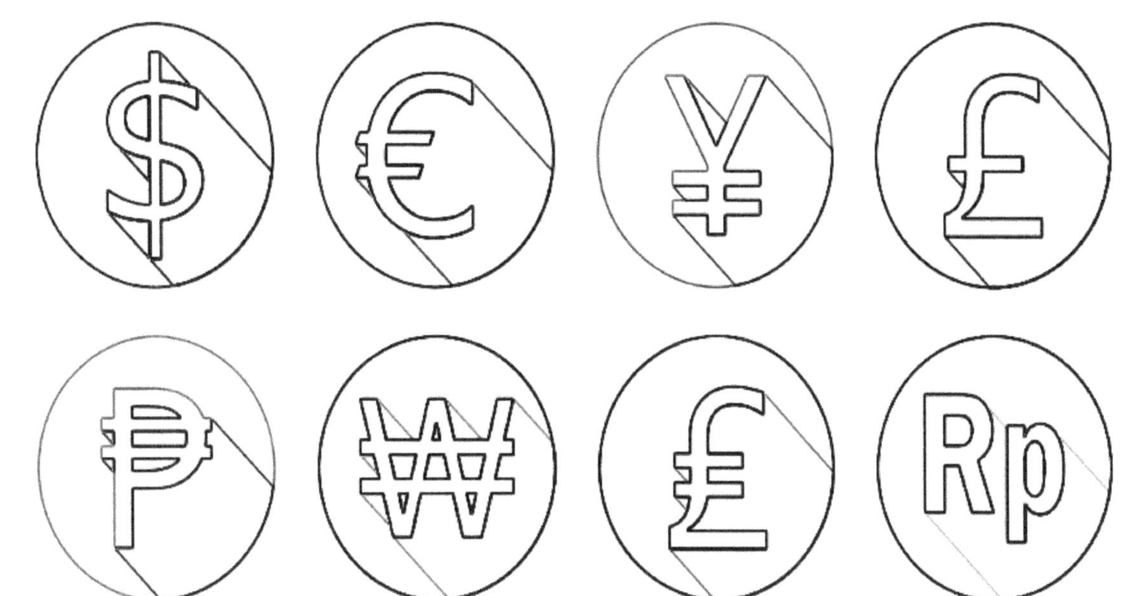

Analysis-Based Trading Strategies

Technical Analysis

As the name suggests, 'analysis,' this method focuses primarily on the evaluation of the market trends through charts as a means of predicting the to-be price trends of the market.

In this method, an evaluation of assets is done basing on statistics and past analysis of market actions like the then volumes and the past prices.

Technical analysis is not done with a primary objective of weighing the underlying value of assets; instead, charts with other measuring tools are used to define the patterns that are helpful in the future forecast in market actions.

It is believed that the market's future performance is easily determined by the past trends in its performance.

Trend Trading

In technical analysis, a trend is a very critical aspect. The tools used in this type of analysis, have a common motive which is simply to determine trends of the market. Therefore, to trend is to move; in this context, it means the way the market is moving.

As we know, the fore market is a wavy and zigzag motion that represents the successive trails that define clearly troughs and peaks which are sometimes called lows and highs? Depending on the available trends of the lows and highs, a trader can define the nature of the market type.

Other than the popular notion of the highs and lows, there is yet another format of the trends in Forex trading called: uptrend/downtrend and sideways trend.

Support and Resistance

It is quite imperative to know the meaning of the horizontal level before defining the support and resistance strategy. This is the level in the price signifying market support of the resistance. In technical analysis, resistance and support as used to refer to the lows or highs in prices in that order.

Support, in this case, refers to an area on a chart, which shows that the interest in buying is stronger than the selling force.

This is revealed through successive troughs. On the other hand, resistance level, as represented on the chart refers to an area where the buying force is outweighed by the selling concern.

Range Trading

It is also referred to as channel trading. This signifies the absence of market direction that may be associated with a lack of trends. It is used to identify the movement in the prices of currencies within the channels of which it is tasked to establish the range in the movements.

It can be achieved by linking sets of lows and highs to the horizontal-trend line. This is to say that the trader is tasked to establish the resistance and support levels with the area in the middle, which we refer to as the trading range.

Technical Indicators

When we talk of the technical indicators about Forex trade, we simply refer to the calculations that are inclined to the volume and the price of a given security.

When used, they are meant to corroborate quality and trend in the chart patterns as well as enable traders to identify sell and buy signals altogether. These indicators in technical analysis can create sell and buy signals via divergence as well as crossovers.

Whenever the prices go across the moving average, crossovers are seen however, divergence occurs only if the indicator and the price trends both move in different and opposite directions implying that there is a weakening in the price trend.

Forex Charts

In Technical analysis, we refer to a chart as a representation of the shifts in prices within a given time frame graphically. It reveals the movement in the security price over some time.

Different charts can be applied in search of diversified information and the skills and knowledge of the researcher.

Forex Volume

Forex volume indicates the total securities by number, traded in a certain time interval. The higher the volume, the higher the level of pressure; this is as indicated by chart specialists.

They can easily define the downward or the upward shifts in volume by observing the volume bars on the lower side of the charts. When a price movement is accompanied by a high volume, it becomes more valuable than if it is accompanied by low volumes.

Multiple Time-Frame Analysis

Security prices must be tracked over a period and in a unique time frame. This is so because a security price will tend to go through a series of time frames, and therefore, analysts need to review several time frames so that they establish the security's trade cycle.

Trading-Style Based Strategies

This is yet another technique, which offers a different way of classifying the trading styles. Through trading styles, trading strategies can be created, which could include but not limited to a buy-and-hold strategy, portfolio trading, trading algorithm, order and carry trades,
It is entirely dependent on your level of understanding, power, and weaknesses that determine the strategies that you will apply. Everyone needs a trading strategy, which best suits his desires according to his ability to apply it.
There is not a style of trading that you must use if you choose to trade, because what suits a person does not suit you and your needs.

Day Trading

This is the act of holding a position and disposing of it the same day. This implies that this type of person does not hold security for more than a day.
You have the right if only you have the ability to conducting more than one type of trade in a single day as long as you do not hold a position for more than one day. This means that before the closure of the market, you must have liquidated all your open positions. There is a challenge in today's trading where if you hold onto a position for that long the chances of losing it are high. Based on whatever style you are using, the targets in the price may vary.

Scalping Strategy

This is characterized by short and quick operations and is applied mainly to achieve vast returns on small price variations. Scalpers can initiate over 200 trades per day with the intention of making good profits on small shifts in price levels.

Fading Strategy

In this case, fading refers to a trade that is initiated against the trend. When the trend moves up, faders sell in the hope that there will be a fall in prices; similarly, they may buy when prices rise.
They buy when the price is escalating and sell when the prices are coming down a notion called fading. It is very contrary to other trends and also to the nature of business.
The trade is usually against the usual trends with reasons such as the buyers at hand may be risking. The securities are usually over-purchased and the earlier may be set for profits.

Daily-Pivot Trading

Currencies are very volatile, and as such, traders may wish to capitalize on that to make profits. This is exactly the case with the pivot strategy.

A turning point, as well as the pivot, is a very critical and unique pointer obtained through the computation of the statistical average of the low, high, and closing prices of currency pairs.

The secret to this strategy lies in the aspect of purchasing securities at their lowest prices and selling them at their best prices in the course of the day.

Momentum Strategy

This is characterized by defining the strongest position that will end up trading the highest. In this case, the trader may drop the currency with signs of dropping in price and go for that currency that has positive signs of going up through the day.

A momentum trader has got several indicators, which help him detect the trends in the securities before he makes his decisions called 'momentum-oscillators.' Such a trader will tend to invest deeply in news feeds which he entirely depends on for price predetermination and decision making.

Buy & Hold Strategy

In this case, a position is bought and held for quite a long before being sold so that the prices escalate even if it takes longer. Whoever does this has no business with the short-term price changes as well as indications. However, this type of strategy best suits the stock traders.

In this case, technical analysis becomes invalid because the trader here is a passive investor who has no rush in determining the market trends of the stocks and securities.

Order-Types Trading Strategies

Trading in order will help the trader to join or move out of a position at the very right time by use of various orders, which include but not limited to market, pending limit, stop-loss, and stop as well as other orders.

At this particular moment, most advanced platforms are fitted with different kinds of orders for trading that are not the common buy/sell buttons. Every order type signifies a certain strategy. You must know how and perhaps when to handle orders before you can use them effectively.

The following are trader orders that can be applied by traders:

- Market order- is put to enable the trader to buy/sell at a ripe price.
- Pending order-enable traders to buy/sell at previously set prices.
- Limit order guides the trader to buy/sell assets at specific price levels.
- Stop-loss order placed to lower a trade risk.

Algorithmic Based Strategy

This is as well-referred to as 'automated' Forex trade. There is software designed to help in the predetermination of times for purchasing and selling securities. This software operates on signals draw from the technical analysis.

To trade in this strategy, you need to issue instructions over the kind of signals that you would wish to search for and its subsequent interpretation. This is an example of a high trading platform, which comes with other supportive platforms for trading.

Examples of these kinds of trading platforms include meta-Trade 4 and Net-TradeX. However, Net-TradeX is a trading platform in which, in addition to its normal functionalities, it presents automated trading through its advisors.

This is referred to as a secondary platform that yields automatic trading and further sophisticates its processes through a language called: "Net-TradeX language."

It goes ahead to provide room for some trading operations traditionally, for example; to open and to close a position to place orders as well as the use of the technical tools for analysis purposes.

Meta-Trader 4 similarly is a trading platform, which makes it possible for the execution of algorithmic trade via an incorporated program-language "MQL4." In this type of platform, traders can come up with called-Advisors, trading–robots with indicators of their own. All acts of making advisors, which include: to debug, to test, to optimize and compiling the program, are all done and made active through the meta-Trader 4 editor. Robots are made in this case to take away the emotional concept of the traders, which in most cases hinders the free and competent engagement in the trade across the platforms. Emotions have and supply a negative attitude to the traders, especially when there is hope for a loss.

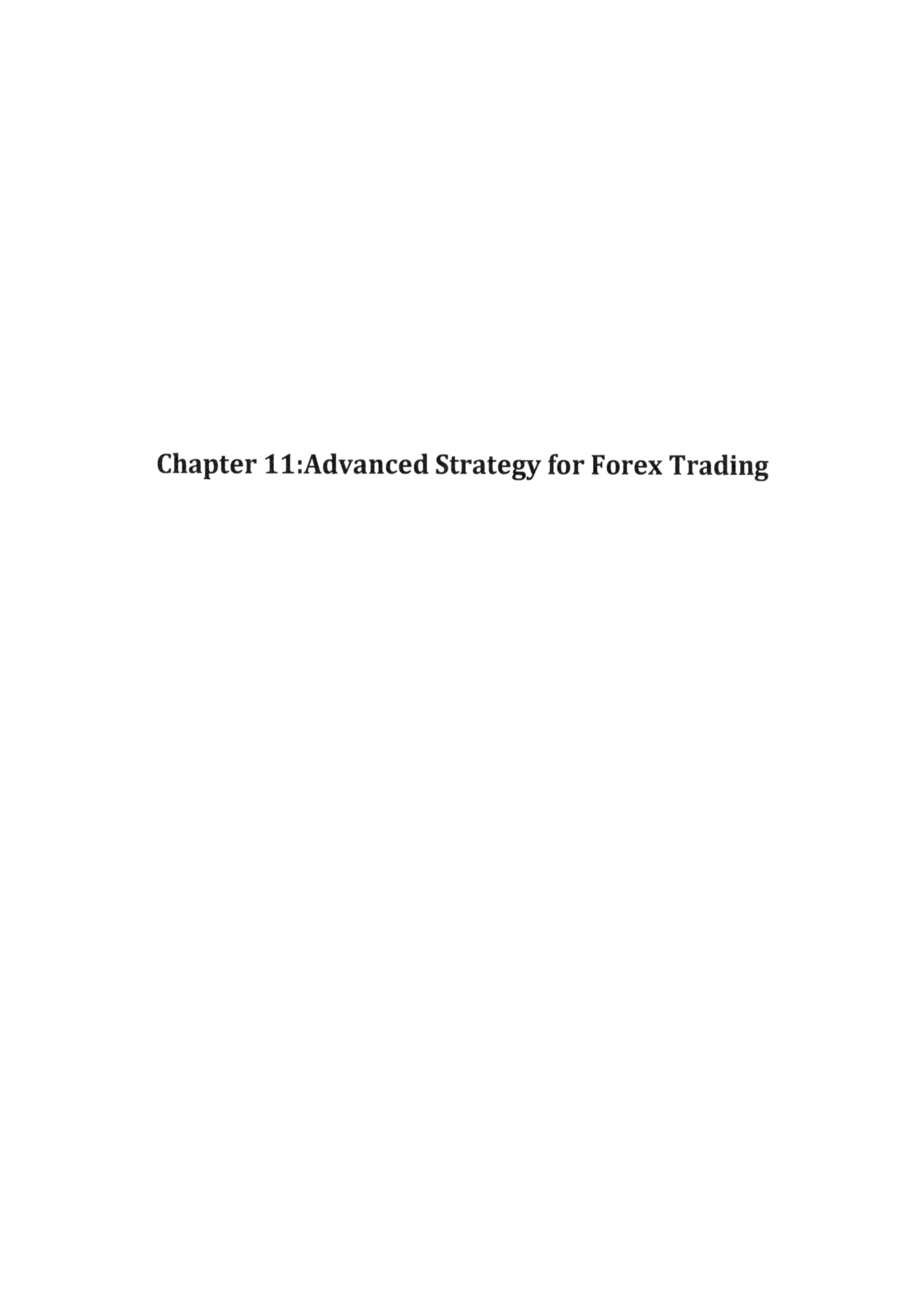

Chapter 11:Advanced Strategy for Forex Trading

How to Create Your Easy Strategies to Start and Make Money?

There are two different types of people who trade on foreign exchange. 1.) Those who have chosen to make a full-time career of it, and 2.) Those who prefer to dabble enough to make a tidy little passive income. The strategies listed here are for those part-time traders and are simple and practical enough to help you get started earning in a short amount of time. Here are the strategies that you may not have even thought about when it comes to trade, such as different currency pairs, the time of day you trade, and additional features you can take advantage of to help you on your way to success.

The Variables to Watch Out for

The new trader should always approach their first investments with caution. You should know the currencies you want to trade and the time of day you plan to make your transactions. We will talk about why this is important a little later. It is also good to develop a plan to make sure you are ready to trade simultaneously every day. Consistency is the key to success. By now, you should have at least a basic understanding of how to read market data and read the price action charts. If not, go back and study those again before you proceed. You should also have a good grasp of the market's function and the different currency pairs and know how to make the best use of the technology available to help you.

There may be many things to think about, but it is possible to make a nice steady income in the Forex Market as a part-time trader. However, as your income rises, it may be tempting to cast your day job aside for this type of income, but I advise you to wait for a while before making such a major decision.

Let's Talk About Time

There is a reason why timing is critical when you invest in foreign exchange. While the market is open 24-hours a day, the trade opportunities will change throughout. Find the time of day when most individuals will be making similar trades like the ones you plan to make. Keep in mind that if you plan to trade only on occasion, the opportunities to buy or sell a particular currency will be reduced. In a volatile market like Forex, rapid changes can frequently happen, so when you know the kind of trade you want and when it is most likely to be done, you can take great pains to be on point when the most activity is likely to happen.

Those who choose to trade at night may find that only certain types of currencies are available at the volume sizes you need. By learning how volume trades are made, you can choose from the currencies available when actively working on the market.

The foreign markets are open 24-hours a day because as the day passes through certain time zones, individual markets have definite open and close times. When the business day closes in a one-time zone, it will be open in another. It does not mean that all markets are open 24-hours a day. This is important to understand when choosing to trade currencies.

For example, the trading day starts in the Asian time zone at 8:00 AM (21:00 GMT). Later, the areas in Australia and Tokyo followed by Singapore. Some of these areas will be open simultaneously, at least for a few hours each day, as they move around the globe. As the one-time zone closes, another will open with a few zones overlapping each other throughout the day. It is this overlap that can create a lot of excitement in the market. As a trader, this can provide you with many great opportunities and many risks throughout the day.

One of the best strategies is to become very knowledgeable about the times and how each zone relates to the other. As you analyze the market, you will eventually be able to single out how other traders navigate these time changes and adapt their forms of trade accordingly.

Other Factors Related to Time

Other factors may not readily come to mind when it comes to trading on the Forex Market. Daylight Savings Time and other time factors can create whole new challenges for your trading practices. Holidays can cause changes in opening and closing times all around the globe. As you study the currencies and the things that affect their trade, you will also need to understand how these factors can impact the type of trades made and when they are made.

You can see how this can have an impact on your trading practices. For example, if you plan to trade the USD/JPY currency pair, you need to know what times those trades are available. A quick look at these markets' schedules to learn when the time zones overlap will tell you when you will make those trades. A Google search reveals these times for the US markets:

The New York Exchange is open from 8:00 AM – 5:00 PM EST.
The Tokyo Exchange is open from 7:00 PM – 4:00 AM EST.
As you can see, these times do not overlap anywhere on the clock. But since it is not enough to settle for a good time to trade, you want to find the optimum time to make the trade. In most cases, you would wait for the overlapping time to trade these two currencies, as this will be when a business is the most active. So, what can you do here?

The solution is simple. The currency pairs see a lot of activity around the clock. Almost every nation with currency in the system will be trading in these two currencies. The yen is actively traded globally, and so is the US dollar. Because they are both very stable currencies, you will see lots of activity for these two throughout the day. So, when considering the timing for this type of trade study, the market to find the most active trade times to make your purchase.

You can learn this by consulting the hourly volatility chart that shows exactly how many PIPs the USD/JPY moves per hour. The times to avoid trade will be straightforward to spot once you understand what you are looking for. As a general rule, the slower the currency movement, the less likely an investor will see a positive change.

Other currencies traded against the USD that could pose a time challenge are USD/EUR, EUR/GBP, EUR/CHF, and EUR/JPY. Of course, many other currency pairs can also present similar challenges, but these are the most highly traded, which increases your chances of making a profit. As you can see, Forex strategy starts with knowing how to take advantage of the time to maximize your profits. The secret is to trade during peak times, where high volumes are being traded to ensure liquidity. Since each currency pair has its own times of peak performance, getting in at the right time takes on a whole new meaning.

Chapter 12:Typical Beginner's Errors in Forex Trading

Overtrading

Overtrading simply refers to a situation where you trade for longer hours than expected, or you invest more money than you should. We have already mentioned that Forex trading can be addictive, like most gambling games. If you get into Forex without having a clear understanding, you may end up making the mistake of overtrading. When can overtrading occur most likely?

When you are making too much money: It is common for traders to keep on investing in a trade as long as they are making money. The right time to stop trading is when you are making enough money. People who are addicted to trading do not get enough of the action. They continue trading even after reaching their profit target for the day, week, or month. For such people, profits do not mean the end of the business. They keep on investing and trying to earn more even if they have made enough profit, risking losing the money they have already made.

If you are on a winning streak, as we said before about the anti-martingale technique, it could be okay to increase your risk and continue investing. But, first of all, you must understand this technique. Then you must include it in your trading plan with written rules; you must test it, and above all, you must follow it also during losing streaks of trades. Most of the time, traders act this way not because they are following a trading plan, but because they are following their greed.

To ensure that you avoid overtrading, you need to set your trading hours. Forex is a 24-hour business. This means that you can trade at any time of the day at any place you are. To avoid the temptation to continue trading even when you are tired, set your trading hours. You should also ensure that your trading hours occur at a time when you are free. Most people who overtrade combine their trading with other activities. If you continue trading at a time when you should be busy doing another activity, you may find that the combination of multiple activities takes away your ability to trade properly due to the lack of focus.

When you are making losses: The other scenario where people get involved in overtrading is when they are making losses. Losses are very enticing. It is dangerous for a person to start making losses when there is still a lot of money in his or her trading account. For instance, if you funded your USD with $10,000 and set your investment risk at 2%, you may think that your investments are insignificant. In this case, after losing the first $200, you may think that you can recoup your money. While it is okay to try to recover lost money, you should not rely on impulse and emotions when making such critical trade decisions. Your impulse will tell you to reinvest immediately. Most people invest huge sums of money in the hope that they can recoup their money in the shortest time possible. The more money you lose, the more confused you get. Your mind loses control, and you eventually start making choices that are not rational.

This overtrading mistake can be avoided if you take a break. After closing a trade, whether it leads to profit or loss, you should take some time away from the screen. This is a matter of discipline. You should make up your mind to ensure that you control your actions and make trade decisions that will positively impact your life. You must learn to accept and deal with losses since they are part of the business.

When you have too much time: The other reason why people engage in overtrading is that they have too much time on their hands. They say, "An idle mind is the devil's workshop." While Forex trading is a good and positive venture that can earn you a handsome amount of money, you should not spend your entire day thinking about the trade. As we have observed, Forex markets operate 24 hours a day. You may be fooled to think that trading around the clock is the best option for you. In reality, you should avoid trading for long hours. Even if you have plenty of time on your hands, you should try as much as possible to stick to your chosen trading hours. Engage in other activities after trading, even if it means playing games or watching movies. If you notice that you are getting addicted to your Forex trading apps, uninstall all trading apps on your mobile devices so that you may stay away from the trading platform when it is not the right time to trade.

When you lack self-discipline: The other reason why most traders get involved in overtrading is simply a lack of self-discipline. If you know you are a person who lacks self-control, try avoiding Forex as much as possible. Self-discipline simply means that you have patience and emotional control. You should be able to stop yourself from taking emotional actions. The only way to survive as a Forex trader is to ensure that you follow the rules you have outlined in your trading plan. There is no way you can expect to succeed if you cannot follow the rules, you have created yourself. People who lack self-control are quick to make decisions without considering the consequences. Forex trading is a game of numbers. In this trade, you must be sure that every action you take has the maximum potential of being a success. If you start making decisions that are not based on facts, you may end up losing a fortune in Forex. As you learn to trade, you eventually stop making errors that are associated with emotional instability. Your discipline will help you stop overtrading or making any other mistakes that you might have committed. To ensure that you stop overtrading, you must first answer the question of "How much trading is too much trading?" Once you know your limits, try to stop when you reach them.

Canceling the Stop Loss and Allow Losses to Run

This is a mistake that is made by both young and experienced traders. The stop-loss order is one of the most important tools that you can use to manage your risk in your trading activities. Unfortunately, the stop-loss order also limits your profits in some instances. You may feel that the price is just about to reach a resistance or support level, but the stop loss point has almost been surpassed. What most traders do is to cancel the stop-loss order and stay in, hoping that the trade may turn in their favor.

If you cancel the stop-loss order, you may result in two situations: you can make a lot of money or lose a lot of money. The fact that you can make a lot of money should never be a motivation for you to cancel the stop-loss order. Canceling the stop-loss order is a big mistake because if you follow a strategy with a statistical edge, probabilities are in favor of the stop loss, not vice versa. Any action you take in Forex should be geared towards protecting your capital and then providing an additional income. If you approach Forex with the mentality of getting rich quickly, you will likely lose all your money.

There are two main reasons why people end up canceling their stop-loss orders:

A chance to make more profits: As already mentioned above, Forex trading does not guarantee 100% success even if you follow all the outlined strategies in this book. With an estimated success rate of 50%-60% based on analytical data, most traders try making a lot of money in a short time by choosing an alternative means of prediction. This means that most traders are more likely to use their instinct than follow a strategy with a statistical edge. While instinct trading can be beneficial, it is also very risky. If you keep on reading volatile news and blogs, you may fool yourself to think that you are ready for the Big Money. Those who encourage traders to make bold moves are experienced brokers. They encourage you to stop following your plan and take risks based on how you feel. Our first rule of thumb is always to ensure that emotions are not part of the business. If you spot an opportunity that you feel can lead to huge profits, avoid it as quickly as possible. What you feel does not matter when it comes to real numbers. If the charts are giving you a negative signal, it is because the odds are against your trade. Instead of trying to win against statistics, it is better to turn to more secure options. The best security option you have is the stop-loss order. With the stop-loss order, you can change the way you do your business and protect yourself from the risk of losing all your money.

Fear of Losing: The other reason why any person would cancel the stop-loss order is the fear of losing. If you are a wise trader, you understand that one position does not determine your final outcome. Trading is a probability game. What really counts is that on a large number of trades, the profits outweigh the losses. Losses are part of the game, and you have to learn to accept them. If one position turns out to be negative, you have the chance of trading in a new position and making more money. The main reason why people should protect their principal investment using the stop-loss order is that they can still engage in other trades and keep staying in business. Being in a position to continue trading even when things have gone against you is the best thing that can happen to any trader.

Not Following the Trading Plan

The other big mistake that is made by almost all traders is failing to follow the trading plan. The main reason why traders should follow the plan is that it helps avoid making mistakes. Mistakes are caused by bad choices, and bad choices cause losses. If you are in a moment of frustration, you are likely to make a mistake. However, if you stick to your trading plan, you do not give your emotions the chance to lead you to lose money. Some of the common errors that occur due to abandoning the trading plan include:

Changing your trading strategy: One of the most important factors outlined in your trading plan is the trading strategy. We have looked at multiple strategies. Each of the strategies has its positives and negatives. When you create a plan, you choose whether to use one strategy or use many. The choice to use a certain strategy is determined by your understanding of the market and your trial results. Before you settle on a trading strategy, it is advisable indeed to try it out and find if it is effective according to your market analysis and if it gives you a statistical edge. Changing your chosen trading strategy midway is the worst mistake you could make. This is not only a mistake because it may lead to losses, but it leads to questioning your full trading plan. The only reason you have a plan is so that you may follow it and utilize it to the end. If you believe in whatever you are doing, there are chances that you will make money from it. In case you choose to change the strategy, it should be because you have observed the market and analyzed it. Change your trading strategy only if you have the data to show that it is better to do so. You should have valid reasons, which can be verified by other traders.

Conclusion

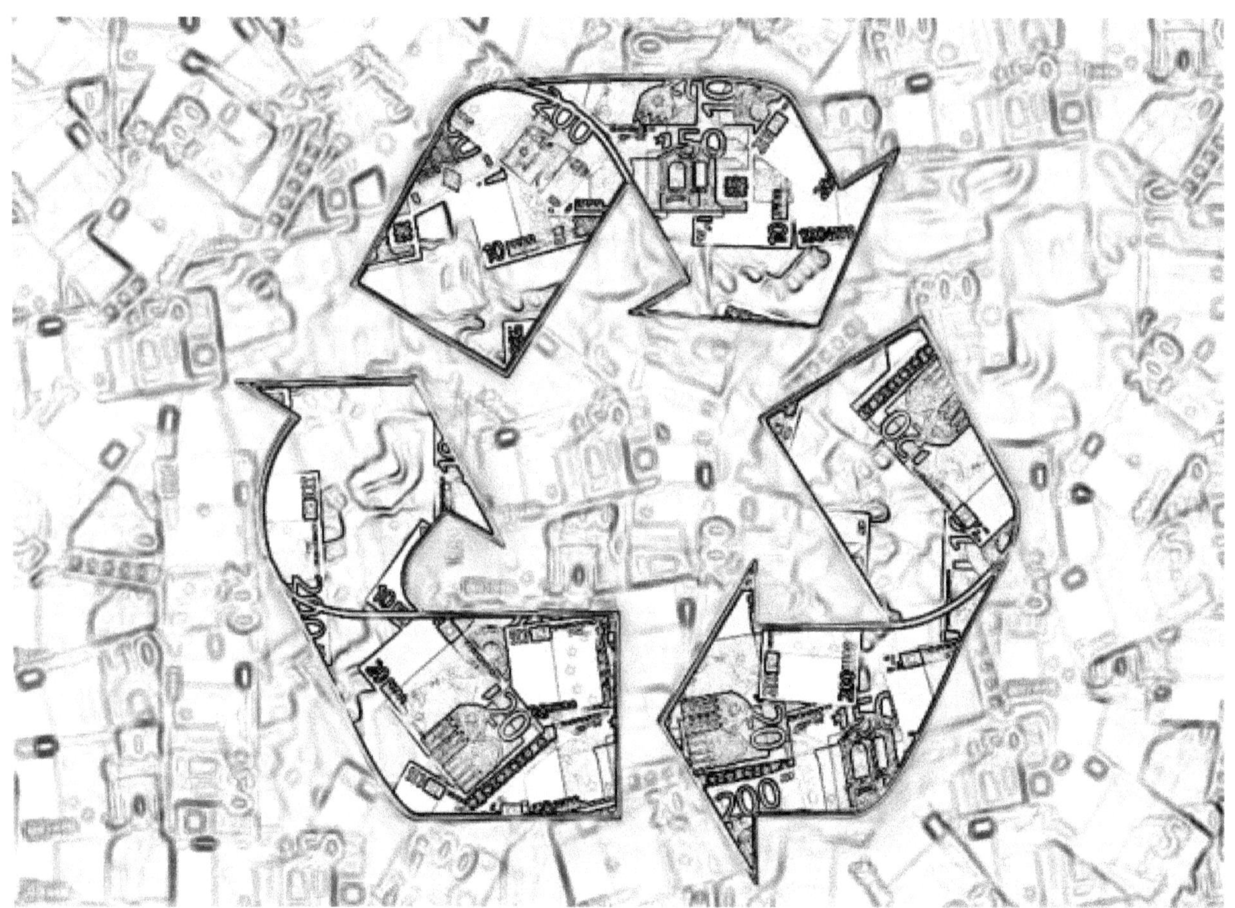

So, what do you think?

How long did you get through this little book? Was the duration enough to help you ease into your new life as a day trader?

If that is the case, then wonderful! Hopefully, the book has provided you with the assistance you need to navigate this new and challenging world.

While I was writing this, I sometimes talked to my friend Ron about how this was turning out to be an encapsulation of everything that I have learned in day trading. While I read textbooks, mingled in online forums, and attended little certification classes, it is a friend's guidance that got me through everything. I am very thankful that I have a friend in him.

But guess what? He likes being in the background, happy that he is successful, at least with the goals that he has set for himself. As for his mentee, yours truly, day trading has afforded me something that goes beyond the usual 9 to 5. I get the excitement of wins and the obvious benefits of earning extra money. It felt liberating to be outside my cubicle prison, at least in spirit. I had been able to extend my reach to something that could help me earn money without me toiling for hours a day.

So why did I say that success was earned, mainly because I had trading friends?

Well, think of it this way.

A stranger approaches you and tells you about this new way of earning money. He wants to have a nice chat over coffee. This stranger insists that you have to invest at least $25,000 so that you can trade with a reputable broker.

Nothing he said is wrong so far. Aren't those the facts that we have talked about?

But he is a stranger. The coffee invite sounds reminiscent of some scammers that you know of.

With Ron, it is different. He did not invite me at all. Instead, he just got engrossed in day trading. Then, his life changes followed. He left his 9 to 5 to set up his business. We got worried about him because he was a married man with kids. He could not just be leaving something that is so sure?

What about pension plans? Retirement? Security?

Suddenly, we saw that life had started to improve. We were the ones who asked questions, and he was ready to answer.

What I am trying to say here is that I hope I was able to answer your questions. I hope that you were able to consider me as your day trading guide, your Ron. Indeed, I am not physically present. However, I wish the contents of this book would have given you a sense of security to find a reputable broker to day trade with.

Are you still in your 9 to 5 cubicle? It does not matter. Nobody is rushing you to do anything right now. It is our decision to make. Right now, though, you have been equipped with everything that you need to succeed:

- Knowledge

- Opportunity
- Assurance

You now know-how:
- To find the right broker
- To identify a good trading platform
- To read and understand the various parts of a trading platform
- To recognize market trends and patterns
- To apply risk management
- To make decisions with or without a mentor
- To play it safe while also being decisive
- To handle stress in the short-period trading format
- To see the science and logic of trading

When to use Day Trading?

Day trading is best for people who are comfortable taking a lot of risks. You need to be able to cope with high amounts of volatility and be able to trade during all hours since day trading is an active style of investing.

Day trading is best suited for short-term traders who follow the markets closely and can take advantage of intra-day price changes.

When to use Swing Trading?

Swing traders typically have more time on their hands than day traders, which means they can either wait hours or days for the market conditions that they want. Unlike day traders, who try to make a few quick trades every day, swing traders might hold their stocks for weeks or months at a time.

If you're interested in market timing, developing a good sense for when price levels will be low or high helps to have the time to wait for the conditions to develop.

Swing trading is best suited for long-term traders who follow the markets. Swing traders like to buy stocks and hold them for up to six months at a time, selling them only if they show signs of deteriorating performance.

When to use Forex Trading?

The world's currency markets are huge and can move dramatically. If you believe that moves in currency rates will significantly affect your portfolio value, you might want to try forex trading.

Forex trading requires more experience and knowledge than the other options on this list, so it's less suitable for people who only have a little bit of experience. If you choose the forex market, you'll need to be able to read charts and technical analysis to figure out trends and pounce on opportunities as soon as they appear.

Trading strategies are especially important in the forex market because it doesn't have an open-ended period of trading. For example, if you want to buy foreign currency at 1:00 today (when rates are high) and sell at 1:00 tomorrow (when rates are low), you stand to make a tidy profit if rates stay relatively flat between those two times.

The markets are open five days a week on average, with some high-volume currencies trading for 22 hours per day. Some currency pairs are only open for a few hours per day, so intraday opportunities might be limited.

Forex trading is best suited for people who have experience in other markets or in trading in general. If you want to trade forex, it's probably best to start developing your skills through practice accounts and classes. You might not be able to afford big losses (or profits) at first, but the more you trade, the better you'll get at it and the better your chances of success.

You are ready. You did not even have to leave the comfort of your home. This book has provided you with a path that will help you journey towards financial success.

Be wary, though. This book does not promise miracles. It only assures you that no matter how seemingly volatile the financial market is, you can make sense of patterns and trends to win at it.

For now, I wish you the best of luck. I hope you will make the most of the information that you have been given. Remember that your patience, strategy, and risk management are more crucial to success than high-tech monitors and computers.